london
museums

london
museums

a handbook
andrew wyllie
drawings by emma brownjohn

●●●ellipsis

First published 2001 by
●●●ellipsis, 2 Rufus Street, London N1 6PE
EMAIL ...@ellipsis.co.uk
www.ellipsis.com

ISBN 1 84166 049 3

Printed and bound in Hong Kong

●●●ellipsis is a trademark of Ellipsis London Limited

British Library Cataloguing in Publication Data: a CIP record
for this publication is available from the British Library

For a copy of the Ellipsis catalogue or information on special
quantity orders of Ellipsis books please contact
sales on 020 7739 3157 or sales@ellipsis.co.uk

contents

Introduction

How on earth does one select what museums to include and what to leave out of a guidebook? First qualification for inclusion was the possession of a permanent collection, so temporary display galleries, up to and including the Royal Academy and the Hayward, were out from the beginning. Even after that, my longlist for London museums ran to about 180, a list compiled without effort and with no attempt at being comprehensive. We wanted around 60 or 70 entries. So how to make the cull? Location was the next criterion: with very few exceptions the museums listed in this book are within the rough circle described by the North and South Circular Roads. Then came regular opening hours: if a museum could only be visited by prior arrangement, it was out. Even after that, the list was too long. How much too long only became apparent well on into the writing, when I found that it had been impossible to squeeze 70 entries into this book format. There was just too much to say about each, too much richness to try to convey. So that's when the exercise of sheer personal prejudice came in.

A group of museums that I was particularly sorry to have to exclude were the many local-authority museums around London. There is one such in just about every London borough, and some of them are excellent. My own local museum at Bruce Castle in Tottenham, for example, has a wonderful social-history collection, imaginatively and well presented. But I could see no way reasonably of selecting one of these museums without including them all. Given that they tend to be very similar to one another, and given pressures of time and space, I had to make the decision to exclude them all. By way of compensation for that exclusion, perhaps I can just remind everybody of how good many local-authority museums are these days. If you haven't been to your local one recently, give it a go: my guess is that you'll find it's really worthwhile.

Even for somebody who spends quite a lot of time in galleries and museums in the normal way, the concentrated time and thought spent researching this book has been an unusual experience, and has rather changed my outlook on the way that museums work. I started off with no strong views on what goes to make a museum work well, thinking that as long as a museum was making an effort to capture the attention, that was good enough. I've changed my mind now. There are polarities which I would describe as intense curatorship at one end of the spectrum, and respectful hands-off at the other. The former is characterised by a determination to let nothing distract from a complete audio-visual experience, so natural light is excluded, and pathways through the installation are as restrictive as possible, while the attention is wholly taken up with a pre-programmed experience. This is the dominant style among recently organised shows. At the other end of the spectrum, collections are reverently left alone out of respect for the 19th-century person who first designed the lay-out or collected the stuff or whatever – the Victorian Society approach, you might say.

Both approaches have their merits as means of presenting small parts of a collection. The intensely curated installations are very well in their way, though their nature prevents the architecture of the buildings in which they take place from being appreciated, and loud audio installations are a terrible distraction when one is trying to see what there is to see in a given gallery. Just leaving things as they are, on the other hand, assumes that a series of display cases full of mute objects with very limited labelling is somehow going to convey something to the visitor. I think something between the two extremes works best, and the most successful example that I can think of is the Ritblat Gallery at the British Library.

You will need a decent street map in order to find the museums in this book – I recommend the *London A–Z*. London is divided into six concentric zones for the purposes of public transport. Only one of the museums listed in this book lies as far out as zone 5 (the Museum of Rugby at Twickenham), and the large majority are in zone 1. For travel beyond Central London, say the area bounded by the Circle Line, buy a Travelcard, which will cover travel by bus, underground, Docklands Light Railway, or normal rail within the zones for which your card is valid. Often, buses are the most agreeable means of getting about, but their use can be rather complicated, and so I've generally taken the view that if you're competent to travel by bus then you don't need my help. Taxis are generally quite good, but they work out prohibitively expensive for most of us to use regularly. Thus, in most cases, directions for getting to a given museum assume that you are travelling by underground. A few museums are only accessible by overground railway (i.e. run by neither London Transport nor the Docklands Light Railway). Nowadays, these are run by a confusing melange of operators, and I've used the term 'rail' to encompass the lot.

While admission to many of the best of London's museums and galleries is free, there are still a considerable number which charge. In particular, at the time of writing, all the South Kensington museums impose entry charges – which is a national disgrace – although the government may soon persuade the directors that their better interests would be served by accepting grant aid sufficient to enable them to stop charging. For anyone who visits a lot of London galleries and museums frequently, it may well make sense to join the National Art Collections Fund. This isn't supposed to operate as a bargain basement, being instead a worthy organisation established to bolster the purchasing power of many museums' and galleries' acquisition funds. The fact is, however, that for an annual subscription of £27, NACF members get free admission to all the South Kensington museums, the Maritime Museum and Royal Observatory, the Imperial War Museum and the RAF Museum, as well as many smaller establishments in London and elsewhere in the country.

The practical details in each entry are as accurate as I can get them at the time of writing. Things will change, especially where major redevelopment is under way – as at the British Museum, for example. So don't blame me if things have moved from where I say they are. But also, please remember that opening times may change, so it is always worth phoning to check before you set out for a museum. This is trebly so in the case of smaller establishments, especially where a significant journey is involved.

NOTE CE = Common Era (or AD); BCE = Before Common Era (or BC)

west london

Kew Bridge Steam Museum

ADDRESS Green Dragon Lane, Brentford, Middlesex TW8 0EN (020 8568 4757)
WEBSITE www.cre.canon.co.uk/~davide/kbsm
OPEN daily 11.00–17.00 (engines under steam weekends and bank-holiday Mondays)
ADMISSION £3.00 (£4.00 when under steam), concessions £2.00 (£3.00), children 5–15 years £1.00 (£2.00)
GETTING THERE rail from Waterloo to Kew Bridge

The steam-powered pumping engines here are magnificent, especially when under steam, as happens every weekend and at odd other times. Even when sitting there motionless, this collection of beam engines from the 1850s through to about 1920 is splendid. Especially so are the 90-inch and 100-inch beam engines that were in operation on site here from the middle of the 19th century, the latter being 'probably the largest Cornish engine now in existence'. These are housed in a fine 1840s pump house, and are on a gigantic scale. From ground level, they stretch about 40 feet up, and the beams must each be about 30 feet long, supported on massive cast-iron Doric columns. There are stairs so that you can view each of the engines at beam level as well as from the ground. The 90-inch engine is still regularly under steam: sadly the 100-inch one is not at present in a condition for this to happen. To give some idea of the size of the thing, the beams of the 90-inch are composed of two linked 12-ton cast-iron plates, forming the top-knot of this Brobdingnagian contraption, built in 1846, and pumping 6.5 million gallons per day in its day.

In a neighbouring building, half a dozen other beam engines have been installed, brought here from other pumping stations around the country. All are splendid in their way, especially when in motion. A small narrow-gauge railway runs round the perimeter of the site, and the two small locomotives which live here do their stuff on about two weekends per month through the year. The engines are very much the centre of attention, and there are odd, neglected corners of the museum, which have acquired peculiar bits of old furniture, and the carcasses of old bicycles – left to rot simply because they aren't steam-powered, I suspect. Like many places inhabited by mechanical engineers, a spirit of placid tinkering pervades the atmosphere.

Elsewhere in the museum there is a desultory display of diesel-powered engines, tucked away in a shack lurking behind the magnificent landmark standpoint tower of 1867. Back in the main building, there is also an excellent exhibition on the history of London's water supply and sewage disposal – a much more interesting story than perhaps it sounds. Water pipes from Roman London through to the present day are on show, together with a selection of domestic gadgetry associated with water – lavatories, washing machines and so on, mainly from the 19th and 20th centuries. The sewers are the main attractions, of course, and there are good storyboards with worthwhile technical detail, but the installation manages also to be quite child-oriented, with lots of hands-on interactive stuff. Horribly convincing rats scutter in one of the sewage-pipe installations, and I still don't see how they contrived this effect.

There are lavatories on site, a small café operates at weekends only, and the shop at the front of the museum stocks a mixture of serious engineering books and souvenir stuff.

Leighton House

ADDRESS 12 Holland Park Road,
London W14 8LZ
(020 7602 3316)
OPEN daily except Tuesday,
11.00–17.30

ADMISSION free
GETTING THERE underground to
High Street Kensington, then
walk (10 minutes)

The great thing about Leighton House is not so much the collection of pictures as the Arab Hall. This wonderful cool chamber has a mosaic floor with a fountain in the middle, while the walls are all covered in mosaics and 16th-century tiles. The effect is convincingly reminiscent of a really outstanding Moorish interior – the Generalife at Granada, for example – though on a much smaller scale.

Elsewhere, the house has a considerable number of paintings by Leighton (Frederic, 1st Baron Leighton of Stretto, 1830–96) and others. Upstairs in the studio there are a number of largely indifferent pre-Raphaelite paintings. Notable however is Edward Burne-Jones' portrait of Georgiana Burne-Jones, a haunting face which prefigures an essentially 20th-century nightmare.

Linley-Sambourne House

ADDRESS 18 Stafford Terrace, London W8 (The Victorian Society, 0208 994 1019)
OPEN 1 March to 31 October, Wednesday, 10.00–16.00, Sunday, 14.00–17.00
ADMISSION £3.50, concessions £2.50, children £2.00
GETTING THERE underground to Kensington High Street, then walk (5 minutes)

If you want to know what a 19th-century house was really like to live in, then this is the place to come. There seems to be no particular reason why this house should have survived in its original state when so few others have done so – just a mixture of inertia and continuing family affection for the place. There are no individual pieces of furniture or works of art of any great distinction, but the overall effect of the place is nevertheless impressive, if gloomy. The pervasive gloom is partly, no doubt, the result of colours darkening towards a uniform brown in the course of 130 years without substantial redecoration. Partly, though, it must be a straightforward fact that the Victorians were less keen on daylight than we are. Using stained glass in the south-facing windows, and covering the walls with gilded imitation Spanish leather cannot have done much to brighten the place up. Though there are mirrors nearly everywhere, which may have helped.

In the dining room and the drawing room, members of the Victorian Society are on hand to tell you all (and I mean all) about everything. In the other rooms, you're on your own. Don't miss the lovely little courtyard garden at the back of the house or, especially, the bathroom on the 2/3 floor mezzanine, whose walls are lined with photographs by Edward Linley-Sambourne, the original owner of the house. A query here: is it possible to be both unself-conscious and yet amazingly camp? Judging by Linley-Sambourne's self-portraits it is indeed possible, while the pictures of the rather jolly naked ladies tend to confirm the impression that Linley-Sambourne was a distinctly odd man. There are some great photographs on the walls here and there throughout the house – worth looking out for.

Public Record Office

ADDRESS Ruskin Avenue, Kew,
Surrey, TW9 4DU
(020 8876 3444)
WEBSITE www.pro.gov.uk
OPEN Monday, Wednesday,
Friday, Saturday, 9.30–17.00;
Tuesday, 10.00–19.00; Thursday
9.30–19.00. Closed on Sunday,
public and bank-holiday
weekends, and for annual
stocktaking
ADMISSION free
GETTING THERE underground to
Kew Gardens

This is a bit of a cheat on my part, and I certainly wouldn't suggest that you make the trek all the way out to Kew solely to visit the Public Record Office 'Museum', which is really the public thoroughfare that the PRO calls its Visitor Centre. If you are in the area, rained off at Kew Gardens, time on your hands after going to Kew Bridge Steam Museum (see page 12), or visiting the PRO for research, however, then make time to look in at the Visitor Centre, if for nothing else, then to look at Domesday Book.

While Little and Great Domesday of 1086–90 are the star attractions, there is a good deal else of interest on display, including Edward VIII's instrument of abdication, Shakespeare's will, and the amazingly illuminated Anglo-Spanish treaty of 1605. The downside is that this area, open since April 2000, seems to have been designed for the benefit of people with no attention span at all. Disjointed images appear on display boards round the perimeter, while audio/video material is incoherent. Disparate and unlabelled photographs are displayed, and the labelling of glass-case items is exiguous. What, for example is the significance of the 'Cato Street Conspirators' Spikes' of 1820? I recollect that the conspirators had it in mind to kill off most of the cabinet, but what had spikes to do with it, and why are they in the PRO anyway? I think we should be told. The main area of the Visitor Centre is noisy and distracting, though the separate room which houses Domesday, Magna Carta in the 1225 version, and a few other treasures, is more satisfactory.

The Public Record Office is an institution of considerable interest in its own right, being in effect Britain's national archive. Although admission to the records themselves is by reader's card, the public areas still are worth looking at. The buildings here are strangely expansive, with ponds – a lake almost – fountains and pleasant grounds surrounding the inoffensive development completed in 1997. There is a spacious café, with an adequate though unambitious menu. Also, a shop with serious historical books, many of them published by the PRO itself, along with rather a lot of genealogical and monarchical tat.

Museum of Rugby

ADDRESS Twickenham Stadium, Rugby Road, Twickenham TW1 1DZ (020 8892 8877) WEBSITE www.rfu.com OPEN Tuesday to Saturday and bank-holiday Mondays, 10.00–17.00; Sunday, 14.00–17.00. Closed Monday except bank holidays, Good Friday, 24–26 December, match days except for match ticket holders, some post-match days (telephone to check). Tours at 10.30, 12.00, 13.30, 15.00. Sunday, 15.00 only ADMISSION museum and tour £5.00, concessions £3.00. Museum or tour £3.00, concessions £2.00 GETTING THERE rail from Waterloo to Twickenham, then boring walk (10 minutes)

To get the most out of this museum, it is probably best to include a guided tour of Twickenham Stadium with your visit, at a small extra cost. The museum begins with a re-creation of behind-the-scenes, in graphic and convincing detail, with bloody bandages and discarded jockstraps decorating the dressing rooms and first-aid post. There are also tableaux of play in progress and a commentator's box. Then the history of the game is illuminated with story-boards and memorabilia, from the day in 1823 when William Webb Ellis picked up the ball and ran with it, through the codification and consolidation of the rules of play in the 1830s and 1840s, the 1895 split of the northern clubs to form what has now become rugby league, through to the modern union game. (In case you don't know, rugby union is slightly posh and until recently was played as an entirely amateur sport, whereas rugby league is gritty and northern, played to different rules, and has paid its players for many years.) The Twickenham museum is concerned solely with Rugby Union, and almost entirely with rugby in England, at that: Welsh people, it seems to me, might reasonably feel a bit miffed at the near complete exclusion of any mention of Wales from this museum devoted to the Welsh national sport.

The display continues with strips, photographs and silverware, including the Calcutta Cup, though this presumably disappears whenever Scotland win it. There are storyboards and video installations, including a full-scale film on the history of the game and recent international highlights. A rather good display of cartoons and paintings related to rugby completes the display.

There is a large shop, mainly selling strips, and a rather ghostly café, operating in premises designed to cater for the crowds on match days. The stadium tour takes about 80 minutes, and gives you the opportunity to see the 1990–95 stands, which, together with the 1981 south stand, give the stadium its current seating capacity of 75,000, a most impressive sight even when empty. You also have the opportunity to see inside some of the hospitality suites, and various other sites of more or less obscure privilege and patronage. Above all, there is the chance to touch, though not to walk on, the hallowed turf.

Wimbledon Lawn Tennis Museum

ADDRESS The All England Lawn
Tennis & Croquet Club, Church
Road, Wimbledon, London
SW19 5AE (020 8946 6131)
WEBSITE www.wimbledon.org
OPEN daily, 10.30–17.00, except
during, and immediately
preceding and after Wimbledon
championships, and 24–26
December and 1 January
ADMISSION £5.00,
concessions £4.00
GETTING THERE underground
to Southfields, then boring walk
(15 minutes)

Wimbledon, naturally, provides the home for this museum
devoted to the history of lawn tennis. The focus is rather
unexpected, in that a good deal of space is given to the evolution of women's dress over a hundred or so years. But
there is also a range of material on different aspects of the
history of the game, and almost endless video footage of
Wimbledon finals over the past 30 years.

Tennis clothes for women evolved so as to provide
increasing physical comfort and freedom, as is clear from
the clothes on display, from the remarkably cumbersome
gear worn in the 1870s, through to the recognisably functional sporting dress of the 1930s and on. A dynamic must
have existed between the development of new styles of tennis dress and that of everyday clothes for women. Tennis
may well have been a trailblazer in this respect, and indeed
dress serves as a worthwhile symbol for other aspects of the
gradual emancipation of women. Life-size tableaux of tennis
parties in the 1890s and 1900s make the point well: barring
the headgear, the clothes worn by the men could be worn
today without undue self-consciousness, while the same is
absolutely not the case with the women's clothes.

The evolution of lawn tennis from real tennis is thoroughly mapped, with storyboards and glass-case exhibits.

It's food for thought that the invention of the rotary lawn-mower was an essential prerequisite for the development of the game. There is also something faintly improbable in the fact that the modern game should owe its existence to boxed sets of nets, rackets and balls, marketed under the name 'sphairistiké' by their inventor, Walter Wingfield, in the 1870s. A modest installation gives some basic technical detail on the making of tennis racquets and balls. Elsewhere there is a children's corner, and extensive displays of silver-ware. The highlight of the museum, however, is the outlook over Centre Court, looking grimly efficient, even with nothing going on. Meanwhile the low point is the video shown in the small theatre, which seems to consist largely of Cliff Richard.

For the enthusiast, there are storyboard and video instal-lations devoted to the careers of numerous post-war heroes, including Billie Jean King, Martina Navratilova, and Bjorn Borg, as well as a display of shoes, clothes and racquets used by the likes of Becker, Edberg and McEnroe in various championships. (They sign the shoes.) An intelligent array of storyboards maps the transfer of dominance in the game from Britain to the USA, Australia, and Europe, though with-out speculating as to the factors which may generate national pre-eminence in the game.

There is a shop selling souvenirs, sweatshirts, books and videos, and a reasonably pleasant, old-fashioned café.

chelsea
and westminster

Carlyle's House

ADDRESS 24 Cheyne Row,
London SW3 5HL
(020 7352 7087)
OPEN 1 April to 31 October,
Wednesday to Sunday and bank-
holiday Mondays, 11.00–17.00.

Closed Good Friday
ADMISSION £3.50,
children £1.75
GETTING THERE underground to
South Kensington or Sloane
Square, then walk (15 minutes)

This is both a shrine to Carlyle the man, and an interesting reconstruction of a mid-19th-century domestic set-up. Jane and Thomas Carlyle moved into this house in 1834 and lived here until their respective deaths. Most rooms in the building are open to the public, furnished in the mid-19th-century style, and with a number of survivals used by the Carlyles themselves. Additionally, there are several portraits of Carlyle dotted about. On the ground floor, perhaps the best thing is Robert Tait's 'A Chelsea Interior', which Jane Carlyle is said to have hated, not least because Tait took over much of the ground floor of the house for the duration of the many sittings necessary for him to finish the picture. Interesting to note how very much smaller is the house in reality than as conveyed in Tait's picture. There are only two small rooms on each floor, which makes for quite a brisk visit.

Downstairs, the basement kitchen looks impressively authentic, with its dresser contemporary with the building of the house in 1708, and its old stone sink and pump for the well. (How many other houses in Chelsea today have comparable facilities?) Upstairs on the first floor, the drawing room has a substantial number of Carlyle's books on display, on long-term loan from the London Library, while at the rear of the house Jane Carlyle's bedroom and dressing room are furnished sparingly, to provide an effect both

pleasing and rather austere. On the first-floor landing hangs the framed address given to Carlyle on his 80th birthday, a pompous and very Victorian text, but signed by around 120 people including both Charles and Erasmus Darwin, George Eliot, Trollope and Tennyson. The top-floor study has an extensive array of books, and memorabilia in glass cases. These range from a broken pipe once smoked by Carlyle to volumes of letters in facsimile and some original letters and manuscripts.

This is a house with a pleasing atmosphere, partly because the furniture is simple and good, and there is no sense of clutter. Those who are not devotees of Carlyle will have to make a decision as to whether that pleasing interior of itself justifies the slightly awkward journey to get here.

National Army Museum

ADDRESS Royal Hospital Road, Chelsea, London SW3 4HT (020 7730 0717)
WEBSITE www.national-army-museum.ac.uk
OPEN daily, 10.00–17.30. Closed 24–26 December, 1 January, Good Friday, May Day bank holiday
ADMISSION free
GETTING THERE underground to Sloane Square, then boring walk (15 minutes)

The National Army Museum occupies a rather dull 1970s/1980s building on Royal Hospital Road, just west of the Royal Hospital. On the whole, the museum is far more interesting and less triumphalist than might be feared, though this has to be a matter of individual taste and judgement.

Starting at the top, the way up is lined with some not very good action paintings from the two world wars, each of them accompanied by an essay of considerable length. This mission to explain is also evident in the art gallery, which is lined with portraits of soldiers, most of them tedious – though there is a nice dodgy Reynolds and a fine Rex Whistler self-portrait with bottles – and almost all with lengthy explanations of who's who. When I was there, it was evident that nobody ever goes into the picture gallery, and I was viewed with extreme suspicion by the servitor. On the same floor is an exhibition devoted to the role of women in the army, mainly consisting of uniforms from World Wars 1 and 2, though with some interesting storyboards and some communications equipment, summing up the museum's view of the main sphere of activities by women in the army. The current controversy about women's fighting role seems to be completely ducked here.

Next door is 'The Modern Army', a room unfortunately dominated by a propagandist video on Kosovo, weirdly spread across nine monitor screens. In addition to the usual display of uniforms and weapons there are also here an interactive video game on putting a rifle together and installations aimed at teaching map-reading, etc. I liked best the display of rations from recent conflicts, and a mobile postbox from the Gulf War.

Downstairs to the first floor, where there are the main displays. 'The Road to Waterloo' segues into 'The Victorian Soldier'. Both consist mainly of uniforms and equipment, waxworks and informative accompanying storyboards. There is a huge Waterloo installation, allegedly made (completed?) in 1838, comprising a model of the battlefield, with some 70,000 tiny model soldiers ranged across it in battle order. An accompanying film explains who was doing what to whom as groups of model soldiers are spotlit in turn. Less edifying is the skeleton of Napoleon's favourite horse, which sits pointlessly in a glass case.

'The Nation in Arms' is devoted to the 1914–18 and 1939–45 conflicts, and has some quite fascinating material, presented in a series of tableaux as well as conventional glass-case displays. There is a mock-up of a World War 1 trench, and no attempt is made to disguise the misery of the situation, or the tremendous number of lives lost. With World War 2, the assemblage of uniforms and weapons, of tableaux and audio/video material is impressive and fascinating, but oddly uncontextualised. Because this is the British National Army Museum, I suppose, no need is felt to mention the words 'Jew' or 'homosexual' or 'gypsy' or 'political opponent'. A problem which is particularly apparent here is that of trying to mount a comprehensive exhibition in a confined space. One's passage through takes turn upon turn and becomes quite confusing, while audio/video

installations conflict with one another because of their undue proximity. As a result, it becomes rather difficult to obtain a coherent picture. I have no idea what the solution to this problem is, though headphones would help. What I do know is that the endless 'atmospheric' tape of 'It's a Long Way to Tipperary' is maddening and should be ritually destroyed.

On the ground floor there is a small shop and an unambitious café, also a substantial temporary exhibition space. Follow the ramp down to the basement, passing through a captivating exhibition comprising a staff-car tableau and photographs together with storyboards relating to something called BRIXMIS, a British army intelligence-gathering mission in East Germany throughout the Cold War.

At the foot of the ramp is the Redcoat Gallery. Paintings, uniforms, weapons, and waxworks depict the role of the English Army from the 15th century to about 1800, including the oppression of the Jacobites in Scotland and the attempted suppression of the American Revolution.

The lower ground floor has a room devoted to 'Cut, Thrust & Swagger', or swords through the ages. Interesting to note from the antique video on show that Wilkinson Sword, the razorblade people, are in fact 'the royal swordmakers'. The craftsmanship involved in making these things is very considerable, and it would be a shame to beat all of them into ploughshares.

Tate Britain

ADDRESS Millbank, London,
SW1P 4RG (020 7887 8000;
information@tate.org.uk)
WEBSITE www.tate.org.uk

OPEN daily, 10.00–17.50
ADMISSION free
GETTING THERE underground to
Pimlico, then walk (5 minutes)

At the time of writing, Tate Britain seems well on the way to becoming an object lesson in how to screw up a major gallery. Its new centenary wing is under construction, however, and there is to be a major rehang when it opens in mid- to late 2001. It is to be hoped that at that point the more negative of the few remarks which follow will be rendered obsolete. Tate Britain's prime *raison d'être* is now to display British art from 1500 to 2000 (though with the caveat that much of the best British 20th-century art is displayed in Tate Modern, naturally enough). The gallery is currently composed of two principal parts: the main building, designed by Sidney R J Smith, which opened in 1897, and was extended in the 1920s and 1930s, and the Clore Gallery, designed by James Stirling, which opened in 1985, and was largely devoted to the display of works by J M W Turner.

It was always going to be a trying time for the Millbank gallery when Tate Modern opened down the river, and the reality of Tate Modern's huge success has made the perception of Tate Britain's problems all the more acute. What really great paintings, after all, were there left in Millbank after the 20th-century stuff went downstream? To which one sure and certain answer was that there were always the Turners: the largest collection in the world of the works of one of the greatest artists of all time. To my mind, Turner is the Beethoven of the visual arts – an amazing genius, operating far ahead of his time. And in Turner's case, pioneering a genre which was only taken up many years later and in another country. What, then, has Tate Britain done to capitalise on its Turner holdings? They have devoted much of the Clore Gallery to a temporary exhibition of artists other than Turner, and taken off public display the 1790's North Wales watercolours in which the astounding idiosyncrasy of Turner's proto-modernist genius was first apparent. They have also, in pursuit of their new achronological approach to hanging paintings, distributed a number of their other Turners through the galleries in the main building. In short, they have sabotaged the display of their principal asset.

I don't know whether there is any real shortage of temporary exhibition space in London at present, but one effect of the dispersal to Bankside is that Tate Britain now has more than it used to, and some interesting installations are in prospect as a result. The thematic rehang has caused controversy, with some prominent art critics denouncing it strongly. There is the difficulty of finding individual works by a given artist, which I find annoying, but many other people don't seem to bother about. Apart from that, some of the themed galleries are effective, others just appalling ('Roast Beef'. Really!).

Among the Turners still on display in the Turner rooms, *Peace – Burial at Sea of Sir David Wilkie* and its pair *War. The Exile and the Rock Limpet* (1842) are astonishing, moving and visionary. Through to the Constable gallery, where 'Waterloo Bridge from Whitehall Stairs' of 1819 is especially striking. Some of the other Turners and Constables can be found in the room entitled *The Land*. Perhaps the most effective of the themed rooms is 'Painters in Focus', a bringing together of different approaches to portraiture over centuries. Here are six fine Hockneys, including *A Bigger Splash* (1967), as well as three Reynolds self-portraits, of which note the 1775 one in which he is shown cupping his ear. Comparison with the bespectacled self-portrait at Dulwich Picture Gallery (see page 195) suggests that this was a man all too well aware of his own mortality. Stanley Spencer's wonderful *Self-Portrait* of 1957 is also here, as is a rare Turner self-portrait (1799).

Crossing the central spine of the gallery, there are some wonderful pictures in the 'Visionary Art' room, notable among them being Paula Rego's beautiful and disturbing 1988 *The Dance*, and Stanley Spencer's humorous but compositionally startling 1935 *St Francis and the Birds*. Also here is Turner's extraordinary moving post-Blakeian 1825–30 *Death on a Pale Horse*. Next door in 'Word and Image' are Henry Wallis' poignant 1856 *Chatterton*; also Burne-Jones' *King Cophetua and the Beggar Maid* of 1884, Millais' 1851–52 *Ophelia,* together with sundry other pre-Raphaelites and late-19th-century erotica.

The other rooms which seem to me to be especially worth visiting are the Gainsborough Octagon and the Portrait Gallery. The former is a rather beautiful room with a fine mosaic floor. It is not a large room, but a perfect space for the display of the seven Gainsboroughs, all more or less life-size, which hang here. Next door there are some really fabulous portraits, among which my favourites include the anonymously painted *Cholmondeley Ladies* (1600–10), which not only displays extraordinary symmetry between these two ladies and their new-borns sharing a bed, but also conveys a sneaky battle for dominance between the two. Maggi Hambling's startling 1973 *Portrait of Frances Rose* and Francis Bacon's worryingly imprisoned 1961 *Seated Figure* are also outstanding in this room.

Downstairs there is a moderate café and espresso bar, and

the now almost-legendary restaurant. This is a beautiful space, and the Rex Whistler mural provides an agreeable backdrop. The service is good, the wine-list is still outstanding, but the food is unadventurous, especially given the price. Still, it remains a great favourite of mine for lunch. Essential to book, and don't expect to emerge with an intact wallet.

Westminster Abbey Museum

ADDRESS Deans Yard, London
SW1P 3PA (020 76544831)
OPEN daily, 10.30–16.00

ADMISSION £2.50, concessions
£1.90
GETTING THERE underground to
Westminster

It's likely that you will visit Westminster Abbey Museum as an add-on to going round the abbey proper, which is fine, you just pay an extra £1. But in case you want to do this as a stand-alone exercise, here's how. Instead of going in by the main entrance to the abbey, go through the gateway of neighbouring Dean's Yard, and then turn left, where you'll see ahead of you the entrance to the abbey cloisters. The cloisters themselves are extremely attractive, though always crowded, and the museum and ticket office are to one side. Then your ticket to the museum also gives you access to the chapter house and the Chamber of the Pyx.

The 13th-century chapter house is a splendid high octagonal chamber, the roof being supported by a single central pillar. The fine decorative tiles on the floor date to the 1250s, and there are rather faded and grimy 14th-century murals. The Chamber of the Pyx is an 11th-century vaulted space, also with floor tiles, and with ecclesiastical silverware from the 16th to the 20th centuries. The museum itself is rather odd. Church of England ladies guard the door, and hand out translations of the historical material which is on the excellent wallboards in English. The translations extend to minority languages, and in the short time that I was within earshot, I heard expressions of disbelief and gratitude as parties were handed copies in Magyar and in Dutch. But the exhibits are a bit grim. Firstly there are archaeological 'finds' in display cases, but these are resolutely of the old-shoe-and-clay-pipe variety. Then the several *pièces de résistance* are effigies of long-dead monarchs. Custom and practice demanded that the corpse of a dead king or queen be embalmed and then put on display. Reading between the lines, it seems that as funeral rites became more elaborate, so the time taken to prepare for the inhumation or entombment got longer, and the condition of even an embalmed corpse would therefore deteriorate to something less than monarchical. So they made effigies to put on display instead. Thus the bulk of the museum's display consists of wooden or waxen replicas from the 14th to the 18th centuries. It's all a bit Hammer Horror for my taste, but might well appeal to the morbidly inclined and the very young.

south kensington

.

Natural History Museum

ADDRESS Cromwell Road,
London SW7 5BD
(020 7942 5000)
WEBSITE www.nhm.ac.uk
OPEN Monday to Saturday,
10.00–17.50; Sunday,
11.00–17.50

ADMISSION £7.50, concessions
£4.50, age 16 and under or 60
and over free. Free to all after
16.30 Monday to Friday and
after 17.00 Saturday, Sunday
and bank holidays
GETTING THERE underground to
South Kensington

The 1881 polychrome Gothic exterior and interior of the main museum are by Alfred Waterhouse and are simply superb. Cathedral meets railway shed in the huge principal interior, its ceiling panels painted with different plants collected by Joseph Banks in the 1770s, and terracotta pillars embossed with fossil animals and plants. The museum is basically divided into two sections, the Earth Galleries, housed in the undistinguished 1977 extension in Exhibition Road, which function well as a museum, and the Life Galleries in the main building which, for a variety of reasons, function much less well. The staff who do the free guided tours of the building are at pains to remind visitors that this is a functioning scientific institution as well as a museum, but that fact does not explain a lingering out-of-orderness in the galleries, nor yet a sense of sod-you-jackery among some of the staff. A visit to the past indeed, to a sort of late 1970s/early 1980s Britain which one had thought we had left behind us.

In the Life Galleries, the second floor is largely occupied by British natural history, closed at the time of writing, and with no firm date set for reopening – 'some time in 2001'. Down to the first floor, where the best thing is room 102: inexplicably devoted to minerals – more appropriate to the

Earth Galleries, surely – it is the most magnificent survival of Victorian museumship. The room is a huge, lovely, airy, light space with a double row of elegant rectilinear columns embossed with fish, including the coelacanth, thought at that time to be extinct. The original purpose-built glass cases fill the room, and contain the most strange and wonderful mineral samples in overwhelming profusion. And there, for the non-specialist, is the rub. While I can see that the neptunite and tourmaline samples, for instance, are absolutely beautiful, the samples in general are left to speak for themselves, and, being rocks, they tend to be mute. You probably need to know your stuff in advance in order to appreciate the significance of, for example, the Anatolian 'contorted fibrous mass' in the Halides cabinet.

Far more effort to explain is made in the Darwin installation in rooms 105–6, though the theme is partly an excuse to mount a display of stuffed animals. The interactive material is lively and engaging, but being set in this gallery from which natural light has been excluded makes the space rather stuffy and gloomy – the mirror-image in many senses of room 102.

I am far from being a member of the 'preservation at any price' brigade, but it hurts and offends me to see the way in which the dinosaur gallery (among several others on the ground floor) has been organised so as to ignore, belittle and cover up the magnificent architecture of this building. A terrific opportunity has been lost to allow modern curatorial techniques and technologies to play off those of the 1880s, as represented by the fabric of the building. Instead, all natural light has been excluded, the shape of the building ignored, and the space reduced to a narrow, winding one-way traffic system, lined with exhibits, some of which are actually pretty good, but by now I'm too oppressed and annoyed to be able to take them in. The ecology installation in room 32 pays similar disrespect to the building, but the replica rainforest is worth seeing, as are some of the tableaux and audiovisual material concerning human impact on the natural world. There is also an amazing video installation about the Earth, displayed on repeating or reflected groups of 20 television screens together configured in a hemispherical arrangement. Skeletons and preserved and replica snakes and fish are in galleries 12 and 13, while skeletons and stuffed mammals are in 14, 23 and 24. The replica blue whale in 24 is vastly impressive. Moving on, through arthropods and stuffed birds, leave the Life Galleries behind and go into the Earth Galleries.

Most spectacular is the central escalator ride through the centre of the Earth, and so to the second floor. Here, vulcanology, oceanography and plate tectonics are extremely well presented, with a nice mixture of material designed to engage people at several different levels. The *pièce de résistance* is the earthquake simulation, where the floor shakes while screens display video tapes recorded in a Kobe supermarket just before and during the 1995 earthquake. The underlying theme continues with installations devoted to weathering and other forces that shape rocks. Down on the first floor is a display of minerals, many of whose samples appear identical for all practical purposes to those displayed in the main building. The presentation here, however, is more informative and accessible to the lay person. There is also a substantial and good exhibition on the evolution of the Earth and the fossil record, with samples, audio/video, and interactive material.

Down on the ground floor there is a worthwhile exhibition demonstrating both the way in which human activities impact on the Earth and how that interaction is commonly viewed. An impressive photographic and storyboard display documents the production of various consumer goods, and gives an indication of the ecological pressures that their manufacture generates.

At the time of writing, only the smaller two of the three cafés in the museum are open, but it is possible to have an agreeable enough snack, albeit consumed under the marble gaze of Charles Darwin – quite enough to make me watch my ps and qs, believe me.

Science Museum

ADDRESS Exhibition Road,
London SW7 2DD
(020 7942 4454;
sciencemuseum@nmsi.ac.uk)
WEBSITE www.nmsi.ac.uk
OPEN daily, 10.00–18.00. Closed
24–26 December

ADMISSION £6.95 (£12.00
including IMAX), students £3.50
(£7.75), under-17s and over 60s
free (£5.75). Free after 16.30
(not the IMAX)
GETTING THERE underground to
South Kensington, then walk
through the tunnel (5 minutes)

First thing to note about the Science Museum is that it is big
– spread over four large and three smaller floors – and so
you need to plan either to be very disciplined or to spend a
whole day here. Most of the installations are extremely
imaginative and involving, so you are likely to spend more
time than you had initially thought in any given section. The
museum is also very child-oriented in some parts, and this
may make a big difference to your routine: if you have children with you, you might want to start in the basement and
work your way upwards through the new Wellcome Wing;
unaccompanied adults may do better to start at the top of
the main building and work down. The number of school
parties visiting is so large that it all gets a bit noisy and
overwhelming on busy days. Probably best to leave the most
popular galleries – 'Exploration of Space' on the ground
floor, and 'Flight' on the third floor – until after 15.00, when
the school parties tend to thin out. Food provision consists
of an unambitious and not terribly large café on the ground
floor in the main building, a café in the new wing, and a
modest sandwich shop in the basement. There are also a
number of places where you can eat your own food, so
bringing sandwiches with you may be the best plan, particularly since it's quite a walk from the museum to the nearest

decent restaurants (Italian or Polish beside South Kensington underground station).

For the generalist, the most important thing to see is 'Making the Modern World', a gallery that opened in June 2000, and is located behind 'Exploration of Space' on the ground floor. The museum has brought together here 'the most important and iconic items in our collections, telling the story of the industrial revolution and its effects on the development of the modern industrial world'. Well, I'm not sure quite how some of the exhibits qualify – Rover's 1950 JET 1, for example, a gas-turbine car, beguilingly based on a souped-up Rover 90. Others are more obvious: Stephenson's Rocket is here, as is the Apollo 10 command module. What I am sure of is that this is one of the most wonderful exhibitions in any museum that I've ever been to. How to make an exhibit devoted to mass motoring, for example. Why, just stack a Fiat 600, Citroen 2CV, Morris Minor 1000, VW Beetle, Saab 93 and a Hino Contessa on top of one another on a great floor-to ceiling rack, with a magnificent silver 1935 Lockheed Electra swooping past. Nearby sits Crick and Watson's 1953 DNA model. Elsewhere, a V2 rocket, a Model T Ford, an early computer and TV set. You may disagree with some of the iconography, but the overall impact of this collection of epoch-making domestic and industrial gear is terrific.

At mezzanine level there is a collection of superb models ranging from a 1680 model 'believed to be the earliest existing model of a fire engine', through 19th- and 20th-century engineering models of cars, 'planes, domestic equipment and so on – small-scale precision engineering of great beauty in its own right, as well as providing a space-saving means of continuing the theme of the main exhibits downstairs.

Further back again is the Wellcome Wing and IMAX Cinema, opened in July 2000, with changing installations devoted to reflecting contemporary science as it happens. This is a large, distinctly hi-tech building on five floors, mainly child-oriented, and very interactive. While going to the IMAX cinema may seem like an exciting idea, the ticket adds considerably to the cost of the visit. The slightly commercial feel of the new wing is extended by the Mars adventure ride, £3.50 for adults, £2.50 for children. The third-floor 'In Future' installation consists of horizontal electronic screens, perhaps 2.5 metres across, on each of which players can engage with the technology – though to what effect is not apparent. Down to the larger second-floor installation 'Digitopolis', which explores the potential of digital technology in a number of areas. Sound, vision, communications, artificial intelligence, and the fundamentals of digitisation each have a group of five multifunctional stations devoted to them. And they are quite fascinating, even regarded simply as the cutting edge of presentational methods. While here, make sure you have an encounter with Biff the cyberdog, a teachable robot the size and rough shape of a small dog.

Down on the first floor, the 'Who Am I' exhibition is very child-oriented and interactive. Human biology, genetics and biometrics are explored in a series of games and other installations, housed for the most part in strange vegetal pods. The gender game is fun: I seem to fulfil the stereotype of a 1960s housewife ...

Back in the main building, on the ground floor the 'Exploration of Space' section has examples of craft from the 1950s to the present, together with spacesuits and other equipment, models and informative storyboards, as well as

19th-century military rockets (perhaps not major contributors to space exploration). Further towards the main entrance is the 'Power' section, with wonderful steam engines from the 18th to the 20th centuries, together with internal-combustion engines of various sorts in a fascinating installation.

The basement contains galleries aimed at giving hands-on experience of basic scientific principles to 3–6-year-olds in 'The Garden', 7–11-year-olds in 'Things' and for 12-year-olds upwards in the amazing new 'Launch-pad' where principles associated with, for example, the movement of goods, or locks and keys, or with a cable-stay bridge are captivatingly demonstrated. Also in the basement is the 'Secret Life of Your Home', which explains the way in which household objects work, starting off most promisingly with lavatories.

For those with a medical bent, the third, fourth and fifth floors are probably the place to head for. On the fifth floor, the 'History of Medicine' exhibition is huge, and offers a comprehensive insight from Mesopotamian and Egyptian material from 3000 BCE through Graeco-Roman votive offerings, medieval medical saints, the Renaissance perceptions of anatomy to 18th- and 19th-century medical practice and 20th-century epidemiological techniques and policy development. On the same floor there is a small installation devoted to veterinary medicine: with its castrators and dental implements this is strictly for those with strong nerves.

The fourth floor 'Glimpses of Medical History' installation consists of a series of tableaux – some full-size, some not – depicting scenes from neolithic medical practice (15,000–5000 BCE), through Roman and medieval practice, then horrible 18th-century naval surgery, a 1905 chemists' shop, 1930s dentistry, and so on, to a full-size 1980 operating theatre. A portion of the third floor is devoted to 'Health Matters', which again is a huge installation, this time devoted largely to relatively high-tech post-war medical developments, with examples of actual machines, tableaux, photographs, audio/video kit, even complete model hospitals, contrasting 1933 design with that of 1998. Some of the interactive exhibits are great fun, but definitely err towards the medium transcending the message, including the most gimmicky health questionnaire ever. This emphasis on matters medical is evidently the product of a continuing co-operative relationship with the Wellcome Foundation.

Elsewhere on the third floor is the 'Flight Lab', with its simulator, which seems to be a species of fairground ride, costs £1.00 per child and £2.50 per adult, and has permanent queues. There are also a number of hands-on installations, including a complete trainer aircraft, aimed at demonstrating the principles of flight. Next door is the flight gallery, a conventional exhibition with actual, replica and model planes from the 1903 Wright Flyer through to a section of a Boeing 747. There are also aero engines on display, together with photographs, video installations, and storyboards, and hidden away at one end, a super little demonstration hot-air balloon. The most spectacular exhibit is the huge Vickers Vimy twin-engined bi-plane in which Alcock and Brown made their transatlantic flight.

Relentlessly onwards, the third floor also has conventional but fascinating displays devoted to geophysics and oceanography, with really good signage explaining means of temperature measurement and so on. Also an optics gallery with a huge range of glass-case stuff, small to large instruments from 17th-century microscopes to lasers. Next door is the photography and cinematography exhibition, presenting a vast range of still and movie cameras and projectors, with tableaux, photographs and storyboards. Finally on this floor, and by way of light relief, is the 18th-century gallery with a collection of truly beautiful scientific instruments – globes, model beam engines, quadrants, optical instruments – collected originally by George III.

The second floor computing exhibition includes the Babbage difference engines – mid-19th-century proto-computers; beautiful affairs, all cogs and levers in bronze and steel. Then on to the mathematical gallery, doors-of-perception explorations of many dimensions in strange shapes and colours. Next, the Navigation Gallery, a large space depicting millennia of sea travel, with models of ships – galleys, sailing ships, steamships through to modern submarines. In all this cornucopia of would-be floating objects, don't miss the model of the 'Thomas W Lawson', an amazing seven-masted schooner. More missable is the Picture Gallery, where a small selection of pictures from the museum's collection is turned over frequently on a themed basis. Other installations on this floor are devoted to chemistry, nuclear physics – with replicas of nuclear-reactor cores – lamps and lighting, weighing, printing: take your pick.

Unpromising as it sounds, the first-floor materials-science section is not to be missed. Not only are there highly inventive and child-friendly installations on the selection and processing of various materials in industrial settings, but there is also a wonderful steel frame for a house (full-size), suspended at an angle in mid-air, and an amazing artwork composed of 213 layers of different materials disposed in a quasi-fractal arrangement. Other substantial exhibitions on this floor are devoted to telecommunications, gas distribution, and agriculture. This last is one of my favourites because it has totally escaped the influence of late-20th-century curatorship. Starting with depictions of agricultural practice from c. 2000 BCE, it moves forward chronologically to a large series of tableaux devoted to a modern day which must have expired about 1965. Lots and lots of uncabbed Massey-Ferguson tractors of a sort which I can remember messing around with on friends' farms in the early 1970s, and they were pretty primitive then. But the models are super, set against painted backgrounds of a rural economy in which monoculture on the grand scale just had not been thought of.

MacDonaldisation has hit the Science Museum irritatingly in one respect, the 'exit and stores' which turns out not to be an area of spare cabinets and stationery, but a bookshop and a toy/souvenir shop. For those who still have the energy, the museum has its own post office at the exit, from which specially franked cards and letters can be sent.

Victoria & Albert Museum

ADDRESS Cromwell Road,
London SW7 2RL
(020 7942 2000)
OPEN daily, 10.00–17.45
ADMISSION £5, under-17s and
over-60s, students, unemployed,
disabled and helpers free. Free to
all after 16.30
GETTING THERE underground to
South Kensington, then walk
through pedestrian tunnel

Behind Aston Webb's remarkable façade on the Cromwell Road, the Victoria and Albert's enormous collections of the decorative arts from all places and all ages are housed in a hybrid gothic structure of huge exuberance. Again and again I find myself stopping dead as contrasting architectonic elements come together to form arresting backdrops to the exhibits. Size mattered to these Victorians, and the result here is daunting, even with the closure until 2002 of the British galleries, so take time to consult the floorplan before setting off into the unknown.

Best, perhaps, to start in the Henry Cole wing, in order to acclimatise yourself gradually, also to lock into your memory the location of the agreeable and spacious self-service restaurant on the ground floor. Take the lift to the top floor, where you will find a fine collection of late-19th-century English paintings, with some super Constable sketches, and a substantial group of Rodin sculptures. It is the view out of the window that really takes the breath away, however, with the V & A's roofscape easily out-Gormenghasting the BBC's effort as it grabs your imagination by the throat. From this wonderful space, down one floor to the Print Study Room, and down again to the fourth floor. Here hangs the Sheepshanks collection of mainly sentimental late-19th-century paintings hung in Victorian three-decker profusion, which luckily makes it impossible to see them, but provokes

the thought: how could the Victorians bear to have their visual arts thus? On the same floor are some important Italian Renaissance paintings in the Ionides Collection; also Blake's *Virgin and Child*. Down again, to the temporary exhibition space and the Frank Lloyd Wright Gallery, and on to the European Ornament Gallery with the wonderful black and white pop-art guitar – only it's dated 1623.

Now may be the moment to brace yourself with a cup of coffee in the Gamble Room, one of three superbly over-the-top tiled rooms, originally designed as refreshment rooms for the museum. Moving on, I love the Swabian 16th-century painted limewood figure of 'Christ Riding on an Ass' in room 27, but in general the question of how much to miss of the ground-floor rooms devoted to the applied and decorative arts of Italy, Northern Europe, Japan, China, Korea and Islam must be a matter of individual taste. Do not, however, be tempted to pass by the unpromisingly-titled Plaster Casts Galleries. In the midst of the most extraordinary gathering of moulds of mainly Classical sculpture sits Trajan's Column – full-size, though of necessity cut in half, and offering the detail which the last hundred years of exhaust fumes have eroded from the original. On now for a short rest in the glorious Pirelli Garden, with its fountain and benches, and take a moment to look at the fine brick walls of the gallery, with their inlaid panels.

The V & A has the largest collection of Indian art outside the sub-continent itself, and selections from this are displayed in rotation in the Nehru Gallery of Indian Art, wonderful small paintings like jewels as well as actual jewels and fine carved artefacts. Also here is Tippoo's Tiger, a remarkable anti-imperialist sculpture of a European being mauled by a tiger, to the accompaniment of a built-in organ designed to reproduce the sounds of roars and screams. Oddly, since the museum's marketing department makes much of this sculpture, it is extremely poorly displayed at present, at one end of an overcrowded display case. Also in this gallery is an amazing Akali turban which, with its sharp-edged quoits, may have been the inspiration for Odd-job's hat in *Goldfinger*. Before moving on, look up – the ceiling is breathtakingly high, and beautifully ornate.

Next door is the costume gallery, the one part of the museum where you are likely to encounter crowds of other people. It is housed in the most superb domed space, a huge rotunda, in which the costume displays seem to stand around rather uneasily. But that doesn't seem to put off the men and women who come and stand captivated by these displays of clothes from the 16th century to the late-20th – how quickly one forgets! But do notice the gender division in front of the various displays.

The upper level of this same rotunda houses the musical-instruments collection: a wonderful range of beautiful things, and an object lesson in how to achieve a compact display in an imaginative and effective way.

Back downstairs and round the corner to the Raphael Cartoon Gallery, a huge beautiful, grey space that reminds me of Grand Central Station, only with no people and with damn great paintings on the walls. And, just in case you were feeling at all complacent, now look back at the floor-plan and see the small corner of the whole represented by this room.

Now to the first floor, and a choice as to how much you can cope with of ironwork, stained glass, metalwork, armour ... The textile collection is vast, a reference collection for specialists, but it comprises gallery upon gallery not

only of display cases, but of closely-ranked racks of drawers and frames. See the Tutankhamun shirt, though, and the collection of 20th-century textile design.

The high-security jewellery gallery offers a weird experience and the reflection that the essentials of vulgar display remain untouching and stony through the ages, however much respect the craftspersonship of some of the pieces inspires, as does the sheer chutzpah involved in wearing some of those rings – *Ave*, Dame Edith.

Don't miss the silver galleries: of course some of the stuff is ugly, but the presentation is wonderfully imaginative, with an interactive computer display of contemporary jewellers' work, and a startling 'what is it?' section.

The 20th-century design galleries are great – domestic gear, furniture, clothes, even the car advertising is fascinating.

Upstairs, the reference collection of glass extends from the 15th century BCE to the present, but the weirdest stuff is 19th-century CE British. The presentation, though, is wonderful, with imaginative use of structural glass – especially the balustrade. Here also is the start of the ceramic collection, though the greater part of it is upstairs on the top floor. Time your visit right, and you are likely to have the whole of these galleries to yourself, surrounded by seemingly endless collections of Chinese pots from practically every dynasty. Then some remarkable European porcelain and tiles, together with the amazing German tile-stoves from the 15th century on.

Probably time for a refreshing drink now.

central london

Apsley House

ADDRESS Hyde Park Corner,
London W1V 9FA
(020 7499 5676/020 7495 8525)
OPEN Tuesday to Sunday and
Monday bank holidays,
11.00–17.00. Closed Good

Friday, May Day bank holiday,
24–26 December and 1 January
ADMISSION £4.50, concessions
£3.00, under-18s free
GETTING THERE underground to
Hyde Park Corner

No. 1, London must have been a very decent Robert Adam town house until the Duke of Wellington bought it in 1817 and started mucking about with it. It is still very fine in its way, but the additions are grandiose and out of scale compared with the rest of the house. The administration seems odd and gloomy as well, and I wonder if the presence of the current duke in his basement flat creates an unduly oppressive atmosphere to the place.

There is no printed floor-plan: instead a sound-guide is included in the ticket price, but of course you can't take it away with you.

The staircase is absolutely lovely, a delicate and beautiful affair, but bizarrely a vast statue of Napoleon (by Canova) lurks in the stairwell, emanating a strange miasma of gloom and pathos. My suspicion is that the statue's artistic merits have little to do with its presence here. Upstairs to the several drawing rooms. The Piccadilly drawing room has a fine Adam ceiling, modest furniture, and generally grimy and inferior paintings, including an alleged Caravaggio. Through the Portico drawing room (I know, it starts to sound like a Posthouse) with its nice mirrors, to the Waterloo Gallery, the principal Wellingtonian addition to the place. This is a huge space, all gilt plaster decoration and grimy paintings displayed to no good effect in a three-decker arrangement. However, there are five absolutely lovely little

landscapes by the elder Breughel, and a really striking Giulio Romano *Virgin and Child*, as well as Goya's celebrated portrait of Wellington on horseback. Otherwise, many of the paintings have a rather dodgy-sounding 'studio of' or 'ascribed to' attribution – some of them may be perfectly good, if only one could see them under the grime.

In the Yellow and Striped drawing rooms there are a fine Canova, *Head of a Dancer* and a really wonderful Nollekens bust of Spencer Percival. Otherwise, rather a lot of gloomy military portraits, though including Charles Robert Leslie's apparently unfinished *The Duke of Wellington Looking at a Bust of Napoleon*, which has a remarkable, ghostly, melancholic feel to it. The dining room has an extraordinary over-the-top silver centre-piece on the table, a foretaste of the regimental-dining-scale collection of silver and china in the ground-floor display gallery.

Throughout, an immense gloom prevails, and it is always a relief to find a window, many of which offer fine views across Hyde Park.

There is a shop of sorts on the ground floor, and lavatories and an unstaffed coat rack in the basement, next to a strange video-show.

British Library

ADDRESS 96 Euston Road, London NW1 2DB (020 7412 7332)
WEBSITE www.bl.uk
(Philatelic: 020 7412 7635 philatelic@bl.uk
WEBSITE www.bl.uk/collections/philatelic)
OPEN Monday, Wednesday to Friday, 9.30–18.00; Tuesday 9.30–20.00; Saturday, 9.30–17.00; Sundays and bank holidays, 11.00–17.00. (Note: different times apply to reading rooms)
ADMISSION free, except as indicated below
GETTING THERE underground to King's Cross, Euston, or Euston Square

Apart from its prime library roles, the British Library also functions as a magnificent museum in several respects, with galleries and display areas devoted to historic books and manuscripts, book manufacture, and philately. It is in any case a building well worth visiting in its own right. Designed by Colin St John Wilson and completed in 1997, it is an enormous functional improvement on the old British Museum Reading Rooms. It also has a level of quality in its interior specification, from desks and chairs to cutlery, which is virtually unmatched in any British public building erected since the war. Unfortunately, financial cutbacks in the 1980s resulted in it having far less reading-room space than it ideally requires, but that is a minor niggle in the context of a truly great building, providing a tremendous public service.

Standing in the rather forbidding forecourt, it is worth remembering that you are on top of the deepest basement in London, housing twelve million volumes, and extending about as far down as what you can see goes up. The interior of the building is magnificent in any case, and although you need a reader's pass to get in to the reading rooms, there is

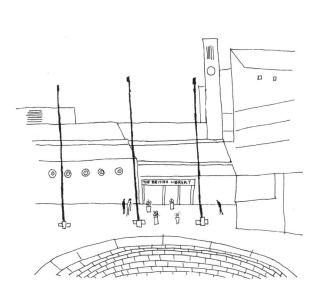

still much that is open to the general public. At the core of the building is the book tower, a glass structure about 20 metres high housing the King's Library, a collection of 65,000 volumes donated to the library by George IV in 1823. These are disposed with their spines facing outwards through the glass, to rather odd effect, but it makes the many fine bindings visible. Around the tower, the large atrium is a splendid space in marble, brick, glass and steel.

Pause for a moment to pay respects to Roubiliac's full-size statue of Shakespeare, and the 7 x 7 metre 'If not, not' tapestry, then turn left into the Ritblat Gallery. This is where the permanent exhibition of particular treasures from the Library's collections is displayed, and it is quite remarkable. Although the exhibits are rotated to some extent, you are pretty certain to see a Gutenberg bible (or two), *Magna Carta* (or three versions thereof dating from 1215 to 1225), notebooks of Leonardo da Vinci, the *Anglo-Saxon Chronicle*, the *Codex Sinaiticus*, and much more. Everything is displayed in sensible cabinets which give each item the space needed to look at them properly, and the labelling is informative without being overwhelming. There are manuscripts spanning the centuries, from the Venerable Bede to the Beatles, but for me the most eerily gripping items are those dating from the early middle ages. From the late 7th century, St Cuthbert's Gospel of St John has 'the earliest surviving European binding still attached to the book for which it was originally made'. I don't know whether it's the odour of sanctity or something, but the state of preservation of the book is astonishing, and the sense that this object is speaking to us from the saintly Northumbria of 1300 years ago has an almost spine-chilling effect.

Among the many other magnificent items on display, the

8th-century manuscript of the Qur'an must almost have come from the hand of the prophet himself, and there are wonderful Persian illuminated manuscripts from the 14th to the 16th centuries. My favourite thing, though, is the Luttrell Psalter of 1325–35. The illuminations in this book have a sparky mischievousness, colour, vivacity, credibility, rather as if they were actually impish figures about to run off the page in a Terry Pratchett fantasy. The labelling tells us that this represents the apogee of the East Anglian School, and it raises the question of whether dominance in the field of the graphic arts of the time may not have been so unequivocally North Italian as I for one had previously thought.

To one side of the Ritblat gallery is a small room with a few computer screens. Do go in, and have a go at 'Turning the Pages'. There are only half a dozen books currently in the system, but you could still spend hours. Each page has been digitised, and the system responds to different types of screen touches, to turn or half-turn a page, to zoom in so as to magnify a particular area of a page. Now you can see the remainder of the Luttrell Psalter, or look in detail at Leonardo da Vinci's notebooks. Even, in the latter case, touch a button so that Leonardo's mirror writing is reversed on screen, making it easier to read. This, it seems to me, is what interactive technologies in museums ought to be: it adds to the exhibits without distracting from them, it is fun, and it is superbly designed.

Downstairs there is a workshop of words, sounds and images, with storyboards and video material devoted to the mechanics of recording text, from papyrus and clay tablets through to electronic digitised formats. There are some hands-on materials around, designed to illustrate ink and paper technologies, for example. Unsurprisingly, a certain amount of the material tends not to be there, having no doubt been turned into surreptitious souvenirs. Installations in this area include an old wooden printing press in working order, and there is a hot-metal compositing machine. There is a very good video on bookbinding, and regular demonstrations take place.

The Pearson Gallery is used for ticketed (£3.00; concessions £2.00) exhibitions, displaying different themes based on the Library's collections. Unfortunately, most of the literary manuscripts which go on display form part of these exhibitions, which seems a shame when everything else is free. However, some of the exhibitions are excellent, and in any other context would be seen as representing good value for money.

Back in the main hall, the Philatelic Collection is worth a visit. Of the British Library's collection of more than eight million philatelic items, about 80,000 are on display, housed in sliding bronze and glass frames. Among them are items of great rarity and interest. Across the vestibule, don't miss Bill Woodrow's lovely 1995 *Sitting on History*, a bronze bench in the form of an open chained book. There are terminals at mezzanine level on which you can consult the main British Library catalogue. Dotted about elsewhere in the building are various busts of worthies, and occasional small arrays of exhibits – maps outside the Maps Room, manuscripts outside the Manuscripts Room, that sort of thing. There is a shop, which is a strange mixture of English Heritage and real things. The range of books is limited overall, but excellent in some subject areas – illuminated manuscripts, for example.

On the first floor, the restaurant is a great place to sit, both for the quality of the space, and as one of the best people-watching places in London. The pricing system is bizarre, with some items being reasonable, others outrageously expensive. Poverty-stricken scholars who work in the Library on a regular basis tend perforce to make alternative arrangements. Downstairs on the ground floor, there is a café, with excellent though rather expensive cakes. It also has a tendency to disappear into complete gloom on dark winter days. With a ceiling that high, the lighting problem needs to be seriously addressed.

Unpromising as the British Library might sound as a place to make a museum visit, it is great, at least for anyone remotely interested in books. There are guided tours of the building most days, probably worth the £5.00 or so charge.

British Museum

ADDRESS Great Russell Street, London WC1B 3DG (020 7323 8000)
WEBSITE www.thebritish-museum.ac.uk
OPEN Saturday to Wednesday, 10.00–17.30; Thursday, Friday, 10.00–20.30.
Great Court: Monday to Wednesday, 9.00–21.00; Thursday to Saturday, 9.00–23.00; Sunday, 9.00–18.00
ADMISSION free
GETTING THERE underground to Tottenham Court Road or Russell Square

The British Museum houses one of the two or three greatest collections of antiquities in the world. It is huge, extremely crowded all the time, and contains an enormous quantity of artefacts which simply have to be looked at at some time in everybody's life. At the time of writing, the Great Court redevelopment has just opened, and, after the building work, Robert Smirke's magnificent neo-classical façade of 1842–47 has a slightly dilapidated piebald appearance, like a great lion with toothache. Every one of the 15 or 20 visits that I have made to the museum over the past four years has involved trekking around temporary closures and building operations. Much of the reconstruction is now complete, however, and getting around the place is easier than it has been for a long time. Having said that, an extensive relocation of exhibits and renumbering of rooms has just taken place: while I have tried to keep abreast of developments, you may well find that the room numbers cited below have changed by the time you read this. Also, the new Africa Gallery in room 25 – which promises to be superb – had not opened at the time of writing.

Although the building is basically a hollow square, the layout is not completely straightforward. Thus, it makes sense to look at one of the plans of the museum on display at either entrance and in the Great Court, and take a minute to orient yourself and to see where the collections are disposed. (Insanely, the museum no longer provides free printed plans, a facility which I hope will be restored soon.)

The major drawback to visiting the museum is other people. I guess that the British Museum is on the agenda for a lot of visitors to London who feel they must go, but don't actually much like museums. That alone can account for the antisocial behaviour, which goes on here to a much greater degree than in any other London museum. It is also sheer pressure of numbers, and it is more than time that a total ban on photography was imposed in the museum in order to relieve the difficulty of moving around the place.

There is no sensible way of looking at the whole collection in a day, so what follows is organised more or less thematically, with the Graeco-Roman stuff needing more than a day to look at properly, and each of the other themes needing about a day's casual work. Obviously, a more scholarly approach would require more time. For those who really have to do as much as possible of the place in a single day, then I have suggested some of the most celebrated exhibits throughout. Many of the individual galleries have free guided tours around them at set times of day, conducted by knowledgeable staff, and well worth joining if you have a particular interest in the material on display. One other point – shortages of staff mean that some galleries are closed at various times of day. If something that you want to see is closed off, it is always worth asking whether the room is due to be opened later in the day. Or, if you come across a really obliging member of staff, you may be lucky enough to persuade them to open a room specially for you.

The ground floor and basement of the west wing contain classical Greek, Assyrian, and Egyptian sculpture and pottery. From the main (south) entrance, turn sharp left and head for rooms 11–15 for a more-or-less chronological progression through the Greek material. Although the Cycladic material in room 11 dates from about 5300 BCE onwards, it is the stylised figures from the period 2700–2400 BCE which affect me most, the familiar spade-shaped heads speaking poignantly from a lost, sophisticated, and apparently despairing past.

Moving through the second-millennium Minoan and Mycenaean pottery and bronzes in room 12, and the other archaic material, the 6th- and 5th-century BCE red- and black-figure pottery in rooms 13–15 includes some lively and erotic painting. (But note that some of the best and most accessible Greek pottery in the museum's collection is in room 69 on the upper floor.) Also in room 15 are the splendid limestone friezes from Xanthus, an aperitif for what follows. Room 16 contains the Bassae sculptures. The site at Bassae is extremely remote and hard to reach, seldom visited, and I believe absolutely magical. The carvings are a little later, by about 15 years, than those on the Parthenon, and they were located in the interior of the temple some 7 metres from the floor, so must have been extraordinarily difficult to see when in situ. But one effect of this is that they are currently displayed in the same relation to the viewer as that for which they were designed, that is to say from the inside of a hollow rectangle, unlike the Parthenon sculptures where the relationship between subject and object is now reversed. The metopes are both far more complete than the Parthenon metopes and also smaller. Oddly, the completeness of these sculptures imposes on them a slightly static quality. Nevertheless, they are not to be missed. Room 16 is one of the rooms most frequently closed because of staff shortages, so be prepared to ask one of the uniformed staff when it will next be open.

Room 17 houses the Lykian Nereid monument, reconstructed in a substantial space which allows the vitality of the wonderful sculptures to come into their own. All this, however, is by way of a foretaste for the main event, the Elgin marbles in room 18. The Parthenon carvings are the finest things of their kind in the world – sexy, alive, moving, and 2500 years old. The fact that they represent the apogee of the artistic achievements of classical Greek civilisation explains the extreme sensitivity over national ownership of them. If the British Museum is the post-imperialist international museum *par excellence*, these sculptures are the ultimate embodiment of the post-imperial guilt-trip: how to maintain international collections, ensure the survival of artefacts while still respecting national sensibilities. While there is a powerful case for returning the marbles to Athens, they are at present splendidly displayed in the Duveen Gallery at the westernmost end of the museum. A simple toplit example of inter-war neo-classicism, the gallery is spacious and shows off the sculpture to excellent effect, even under severe pressure of numbers of visitors. Soundguides are available, and there are auxiliary displays, including a superb, lucid computer-generated video which explains the structure of the Parthenon and the disposition of the sculptures around the building. There is also a full-scale reconstruction of a Doric capital and entablature, with wallboards explaining this and other aspects of the buildings on the Athens Acropolis.

Rooms 19, 20 and 20A house huge numbers of red-figure

pots of the 5th and 4th centuries BCE. For the non-specialist, this is all really too much to cope with, especially the huge array from the reserve collection in room 20A. Some of this stuff is gorgeous, but best save your energies, pausing only to admire the magnificent Panathenaic prize amphora in room 19. Room 21 has sculptures from the Mausoleum at Halikarnassos, completed around 350 BCE and one of the seven wonders of the ancient world. Maussolos' tomb provides the derivation of the term mausoleum, and, given the scale of what is here, one can see why. There is worthwhile Hellenistic material in room 22, including some splendid Roman copies of Hellenistic sculpted heads. The Graeco-Roman theme is continued in the basement rooms, with architectural elements demonstrating the essential features of the Doric, Ionic and Corinthian Orders to be found in rooms 77 and 78, and a huge range of over-restored Roman and Hellenistic sculpture in rooms 82–85. The more interesting Hellenistic material, however, is to be found in the Greece and Rome rooms (69-73) on the first floor.

The exhibits in room 69 represent Greek and Roman daily life from 1450 BCE to 500 CE, and are arranged around a number of themes, including women, children, religion, and marriage. The thematic approach is intelligent and helpful, and adds to the assimilability of the stuff on display. Some of the best red-figure pottery of the 6th and 5th centuries BCE to be seen anywhere is here. Note especially the Panathenaic prize amphora with its spectacular horse race (and compare the chariot race shown in its counterpart in room 19), also the celebrated depiction of Odysseus and the Sirens. Both pots are to be found in display cases at the north end of the room. Room 70 is devoted to the Roman Empire from the 4th century BCE to the 7th century CE. The

Roman busts and statues here have largely escaped 18th-century over-restoration, and so are vastly more impressive than their counterparts in the basement rooms (and see also the Roman Britain exhibits in room 49). There are also some fine terracotta and bronze figurines. The most heart-stopping thing in the room, however, is the fiercely homo-erotic Warren Cup (50–70 CE): astonishing that silver appliqué could be quite so ... ahem.

Pre-Roman Italy is the theme of room 71, with the Etruscans in particular depicted as a distinctly jolly lot, whose 5th-century-BCE relief carvings manage to include women on more or less equal terms with men, all having what looks like a good time. The Cypriot antiquities next door in room 72 date from 4500 BCE to 330 CE, and include some particularly fine figurines in limestone and terracotta of the 7th–5th century BCE, and some lovely 1st- and 2nd-century-CE glassware.

The Graeco-Roman material finishes in room 73 with the Greeks in southern Italy. The provincial black-figure and red-figure pottery is noticeably cruder than that of much of mainland Greece, but has a vitality all its own, especially the very striking 4th-century-BCE Apulian stuff. Not to be missed in this room is the 6th-century-BCE Tarantan horse and rider in bronze.

Moving round the corner, rooms 51–59 are devoted to the museum's ancient near-east material, from the earliest middle-eastern civilisations, starting with the people who built the first permanent townships in the 8th millennium BCE. One thing absolutely not to be missed is in room 56, the 'Ram in the Thicket' statuette from Ur, of about 2600 BCE, an incredible survival elaborately constructed from gold, shell and lapis lazuli. There are also some fragmentary but wonderful relief panels from the Persepolis of Darius and Xerxes of the 6th and 5th centuries BCE, also 'The Oxus Treasure' of gold and silver objects from the 5th and 4th centuries BCE, and some wonderful bronze animals from Luristan dating from 1400 to 650 BCE.

Returning to the ground floor, rooms 6–10 and 26 are all devoted to material from the Assyrian Empire, as are rooms 88A and 89 in the basement. The reliefs of the 7th century BCE from the Royal Palace at Nineveh are particularly splendid, especially the Royal Lion Hunt in room 7. However, any of the reliefs, whether from the Palace at Nimrud of the 9th century BCE, or Sargon's palace at Khorsabad in the 8th century BCE, or Nineveh, have a mythological status to them which fires the imagination. These are the names which figure as early history in the Old Testament, and here is the evidence of their reality. It is only the damned cameras which keep my feet on the ground when looking at Sargon's guardian giants – winged bulls with sombre human heads, extraordinarily complete and new-looking and yet retaining in them a sense of having witnessed or caused the most awful events.

For Egyptian material, start in the long Egyptian carvings room (4) on the ground floor. Here are statues of gods and pharaohs from the 19th to the 14th centuries BCE in an astonishing state of preservation, and wonderful animal figures from the 7th and 6th centuries BCE. Also the Rosetta Stone which, although only moderately interesting to look at unless you can actually read the scripts, has a certain residual fascination attached to it simply because of its historical importance.

Further Egyptian material lines the West Staircase up to

the first floor, where rooms 61–65 form the outer range of the northern end of the building, and are devoted to Egyptian archaeology. Unfortunately the mummy's curse strikes here as huge gangs of people crowd round the various cabinets. The excellent and informative storyboards on the technologies of mummification and on archaeological processes are impossible to stop to read unless you magically find a time when other people are not there – perhaps a stormy Tuesday morning in February. Things worth looking out for in rooms 62/3 are Cleopatra's well-preserved mummy and coffin, and on the wall the wonderful painted textiles from c. 2000–300 BCE, together with splendid bead mosaics and nets. In room 64 the pre-dynastic decorated vases from Naqada of 3600–3250 BCE have simple but beautiful painted patterns, and there are also some fine early dynastic figurines and slabs decorated with hieroglyphics. There is rather more recent stuff in room 65, including super carved figures of about 1250 BCE from Abu Simbel.

If you want to concentrate on the museum's Oriental holdings, the easiest thing to do is start from the north entrance on Montague Place rather than from the main entrance. On the ground floor, room 34 is the Islamic gallery, with glassware and pottery from the 8th to the 18th centuries. Especially lovely are the 12th-century Iranian bowls and jars, which have a faded and beautiful gold lustre on a white background, with geometric and calligraphic designs. Among the many other worthwhile things in this spacious and uncrowded room are the 16th-century Iznik pottery pieces, predominantly blue on white, but with a certain rich geometricality which distinguishes them from their Chinese Ming counterparts.

The main Oriental collection is in room 33, a huge gallery on the first floor. Starting at the western end, room 33A houses a great array of intricately carved limestone panels of the 1st to the 3rd centuries from the Great Stupa at Amaravati. Into the main body of the room, where there is an immense collection of mainly Buddhist sculpture of the 2nd to the 18th centuries, from India, Java, Cambodia, Burma and Thailand. Progressing eastward brings you to China – pottery, bronze, clay and wooden artefacts from 4500 BCE to later Ming-dynasty stuff. Dominating the central space of this end of the gallery is a large collection of c. 8th-century Tang-dynasty grave guardians, amazingly well preserved, perfect, sophisticated, and rather repellent. To one side, however, a series of smaller glass cases house some really lovely Song-dynasty porcelain with its mysterious, subtle, blue-green and cream glazes – celadon ware of the 12th and 13th centuries, and a small amount of Ru ware and Ding ware of the 11th and 12th centuries (though to concentrate on this material you may do better visiting the Percival David collection, see page 118). Room 33B is a long narrow corridor with a temporary display which at the time of writing includes a quantity of Vedantic artefacts.

Downstairs to rooms 26 and 27 and you're in another continent. The Mexican material in room 27 includes a lot of apparently rather angry gods. The remarkable female deities represented in stone dominate one end of the room to terrifying effect, while glass cases throughout contain strange, savage gods and mosaic skulls. Next door in room 26 is an array of native-American material from the Arctic down through Canada and the plains to California and Texas. Particularly impressive are the totemic carvings from British Columbia which dominate one end of the room.

Returning to the Oriental, artefacts from Japan and Korea are displayed on a rotational basis, changing roughly every three months or so, in newish, blessedly air-conditioned galleries on the upper floors (rooms 92–94). Korean material is also on display in the new room 67 on the mezzanine floor.

While in this region of the museum, don't miss the prints and drawings in room 90. The museum's holdings of British prints and drawings are extremely extensive and wonderful. Again, they are rotated frequently, so it is not possible to give a flavour of what is on display, the only semi-permanent fixture being the not very British *Epifania* by Michelangelo, a huge cartoon with five primary life-size figures.

The south-eastern corner of the first floor is largely devoted to western European material, and takes us from 1600 BCE to the present day. In room 50, there is a variety of European Bronze Age stuff, with some remarkably well-preserved vessels from the Thames Valley, dating from 900 to 600 BCE. Also here is Lindow Man, still recognisably a human being, preserved for nearly 2000 years in a peat bog.

On to Roman Britain in room 49, where the most striking things are the silver tableware of the Mildenhall treasure, especially the huge Oceanus dish with its striking narrative chased decoration in mint condition. The dominant influence shifts in room 41 to Norse, with the Sutton Hoo ship burial. Unfortunately, the iron artefacts are substantially decayed, though some have been reconstructed, and there are some fine pieces of jewellery in silver and gold. Room 42 reveals more varied influences, with Carolingian, Anglo-Saxon and Celtic material on display. There is some spectacular ivory carving, especially the Lewis Chessmen from the 12th century, and fine French enamels, as well as impressive

English and Scottish jewellery of the 13th to 16th centuries. Next door in room 43, the principal theme is English tiles of the 13th to the 16th centuries. These form spectacular arrays, with polychrome designs on each individual tile, and then the whole fitted together like a mosaic. Room 44 is devoted to clocks, the earliest of which date from the 14th century and are accompanied by extensive technical detail. Elsewhere in the room are watches of the 16th to the 20th centuries, and some magnificent long-case clocks and 18th- to 20th-century chronometers. Best of these last to my mind, is the 'Congreve' rolling ball clock of 1810, hypnotically fascinating to watch as the ball rolls zig-zag across the tilting plane on which it sits.

The Waddesdon Collection next door in room 45 consists of haute bourgeois domestic impedimenta, with elaborate bibelots and highly wrought silver and gold, but also including some really fine 17th-century crystal. Room 46 has European pottery, glass, silver and gold of the 15th to 18th centuries. The spectacular thing here is the 16th-century English silver 'Armada Service' – austere, beautiful and in perfect condition. The relatively small display of European and American applied arts of the 19th and 20th centuries contains a good deal that is eminently missable. However, there are some fine Rennie Mackintosh pieces in room 48.

Room 6 contains the unpromisingly titled 'Money'. In fact it is a wonderful presentation on the history of money from 2000 BCE to the present, from the silver shekel of Ur to the Euro. In the nature of things, most of the items on display are not that visually arresting (though the 1944 British Linen Bank £5 note is quite something), but the storyboards are fascinating and lucid, especially on the manufacturing technologies involved. Given that the coverage is global, and the storyboards and individual labelling quite detailed, this room alone could take a long time.

The Great Court development by Norman Foster is starkly beautiful – alienatingly so, some find. It is a new thoroughfare, as well as being the 'largest covered public square in Europe'. And it is remarkable – a bright, light expanse within the museum, but not entirely of the museum: a meeting-place, where the space itself is dominant as the contents are sparsely located, but a square within which you find yourself unexpectedly confronting Egyptian or Assyrian sculpture some 2500 or more years old, while waiting to meet friends for lunch. (That's you, rather than the sculpture.) The glass roof is a tessellation of triangles, of which no two are the same, each having been computer-cut to the size and shape necessary in order to create the whole.

The English 'heritage' mentality has manufactured outrage at the cheerful colour of the stone used for the new South Portico, an assertively modern reading of classicism. But more striking is the new white exterior of the old Reading Room, visible for the first time since the library stacks were created around it soon after it was built, its old brick now encased in sculptural stone cladding. The building's function has been brilliantly transformed into a public reference library, retaining the Smirke/Panizzi listed interior, not as a mummified relic, but as a useful and used space. Two staircases sweep round the outside, to the new special exhibition space at first-floor level, and then up to the second-floor restaurant, a quite ambitious affair, though with a reasonable *prix fixe* lunch and friendly and helpful staff.

At ground level, there is a large self-service café in two parts, uneasily dwarfed by the space they occupy. It must be the unfamiliarity of the spatial relations in a covered square

that generates the café's feeling of uncertainty as to how to establish boundaries. But where else can you eat a modest lunch under the protective eye of an Easter Island statue?

Elsewhere in the Great Court lurk the museum's information desk and the main bookshop, which is serious and worthwhile. Back in the main building, there is a rather expensive but quite good café. Also the museum shops which, among other things, sell wonderful replicas of some of the exhibits.

Courtauld Gallery

ADDRESS Courtauld Institute of
Art, Somerset House, Strand,
London WC2R 0RN
(020 7848 2526)
OPEN Monday to Saturday,
10.00–18.00; Sunday and bank-
holiday Mondays, 12.00–18.00.
Closed 24–26 December and
1 January
ADMISSION £4.00 (£7.00 jointly
with Gilbert Collection), UK
residents over 60 £3.00 (£5.00),
under-18s, full-time UK students,
unemployed free. Free to all on
Mondays, 10.00–14.00, except
bank holidays
GETTING THERE underground to
Holborn, Temple, or Charing
Cross and then walk (10
minutes). Buses to Aldwych

The Courtauld Gallery houses a spectacular if smallish collection of paintings, with particular strengths in French
impressionism and the works of Rubens. The gallery is in
the Strand block of William Chambers' Somerset House of
1780. Although the gallery has occupied its corner of the
building complex since 1990, it is only in 2000 that the main
courtyard has been opened up to the public, and now,
together with the terrace overlooking the Thames, forms
one of the most agreeable public spaces in Central London.
Tickets for the Courtauld can be bought jointly for the
Gilbert Collection (see page 91), housed at the opposite end
of the complex.

The scale of the gallery's rooms is that of the grand town
house rather than the municipal gallery, and the whole out-
fit has elegance and style. The top floor houses French
impressionist paintings, among which are some very familiar images, including Manet's 1881–82 *A Bar at the Folies
Bergères*, which notoriously features the Bass red-triangle
trademark. Also here is Manet's late (c. 1867) version of
Déjeuner sur l'herbe, which some may feel is a mistake,
albeit a familiar one. Just to whet the appetite, though,

among the paintings on this top floor are works by Degas, Monet, seven important Cézannes, four fine Bonnards, and Vuillard's fabulous small 1909/10 *Interior: the Screen*, a prefiguring of abstract expressionism perhaps fancifully discernible. My other great favourites on this floor are Van Gogh's 1889 *Self-Portrait with Bandaged Ear*, from the frame of which the artist seems to stick out his tongue at the viewer, and Daumier's 1870 dreamworld *Don Quixote and Sancho Panza*.

On the first floor the collection of 17th- and 18th-century painting is of outstanding quality, and includes a group of 12 little Tiepolo sketches and the less familiar, luminously beautiful Sassoferratos. One room is devoted to a collection of around twenty Rubens paintings. Not to everybody's taste, perhaps, but do note the untypical 1613–15 *Family of Jan Breughel the Elder*, absolutely wonderful characterisation in this great portrait. Other paintings not to be missed are Lucas Cranach's spectacular *Adam and Eve* of 1526, and Caravaggio's grisly 1531–35 *Incredulity of St Thomas*.

Down on the ground floor is the small room devoted to European sacred art of 1300–1500. When you've finished with the pictures, do go down to the basement, if only to enjoy the beautiful little winding staircase. The café here has nice but expensive coffee and cakes, and an agreeable courtyard in which to enjoy them. (More elaborate refection is available at the riverine side of Somerset House. See the entry on the Gilbert Collection for more detail.) Back up to ground level, the gallery shop is across the way from the gallery entrance, and is well worth a visit. Apart from the serious selection of art-history books on sale, there are also some superb poster-sized reproductions of paintings in the collection on sale at reasonable prices.

Dickens House

ADDRESS 48 Doughty Street, London WC1N 2LF (020 7405 2127) OPEN Monday to Saturday, 10.00–17.00. Closed some bank holidays

ADMISSION £4.00, concessions £3.00, children £2.00 GETTING THERE underground to Russell Square or Chancery Lane, then slightly boring walk (10 minutes)

Far less grand than Gad's Hill, of course, this Doughty Street house is still a pleasant place from which one would glean a sense of domestic harmony, had anything of the sort prevailed *chez* Dickens. As currently presented, the house is full of material which gives an insight into the turbulent nature of Dickens' life. There is no printed floorplan for the house, so it may be worth investing £1 for the official guide – though there is a collection of information sheets in the hallway in the most amazingly comprehensive selection of languages imaginable.

On the top floor, there is a comparatively sparse collection of furniture, with drawings, paintings, manuscripts and reading copies of the books (copies prepared by Dickens himself for public readings of his works – instructively adapted for the purpose): also photographs, including those concerned with Dickens' involvement with amateur dramatics – when did the man find time for sleep? All this memorabilia is accompanied by exceptionally informative labelling.

Down one floor, the drawing room has been restored to a state comparable with that in which it would have been in Dickens' day, while the study houses in glass cases a collection of 'plagiarisms and piracies' – contemporary efforts to cash in on Dickens' works – together with draft illustrations for the books.

Down again, to the ground floor, where there is a collec-

tion of some pleasing pieces of furniture, crockery and glass-ware used by Dickens. In the Morning Room is an amazing family tree of the Dickens family, evidently kept up to date in a remorseless manner. Also some fascinating biographical material, especially relating to Dickens' separation from his wife. The basement has one or two pieces of below-stairs domestic paraphernalia, but its main attraction is the 'National Dickens Library', an impressive collection of orig-inal archival material as well as every imaginable commen-tary on and edition of the works.

The ground-floor shop is tiny, but unusually it sells good secondhand books (Dickens-oriented, of course) as well as some new books and the usual tat. There are no visible lava-tories, nor any kind of refreshment provision, nor is the neighbourhood a particular oasis, especially at weekends. So be prepared.

Gilbert Collection

ADDRESS Somerset House, Strand, London WC2R 1LN (020 7420 9400)
OPEN Monday to Saturday, 10.00–18.00; Sunday and bank-holiday Mondays, 12.00–18.00. Closed 24–26 December and 1 January
ADMISSION £4.00 (£7.00 jointly with Courtauld Gallery), UK residents over 60 £3.00 (£5.00), under-18s, full-time UK students, unemployed free. Free to all on Mondays, 10.00–14.00, except bank holidays
GETTING THERE underground to Holborn, Temple, or Charing Cross and then walk (5 or 10 minutes). Buses to Aldwych

This peculiar display of opulent oddities opened in May 2000 in the riverine wing of Somerset House. The promising-looking new concrete, glass and steel entrance lobby is perhaps the best thing about it, unless you are a particular connoisseur of silverware, snuffboxes, or Italian micromosaics. One thing not to be missed is the full-scale mock-up of the office of the donor, Sir Arthur Gilbert, a California rococo number, with much satin and marble – and a wax-work of Sir Arthur himself, resplendent in tennis kit, in the middle of it all. A further room is devoted to a megalomaniac depiction of the life of our friend. (Turn hard left in front of the ticket-desk for this.)

Much of the collection consists of 19th- and 20th-century Italian micromosaics, hugely skilful, no doubt, but artistically negligible. The silver collection is magnificent, and the 16th- and 17th-century pieces are very fine and rare. Personally, I find the overblown 18th- and 19th-century pieces unspeakable, but this is manifestly a splendid collection of them. Among the bibelots, a great deal of craftsmanship is evident: transcendently so in the case of the gold-ornamented boxes made for Frederick the Great in the

1760s (room 8). Otherwise, there is a pervasive feeling of lifelessness, enhanced by the presentation of the collection in a series of small, dim, cube-like rooms, all with a funny smell. Worth looking at in all this are Denis Browell Murphy's 1804 miniature portrait group of the Royal House of Stuart, dissipation and madness refreshingly evident (room 11). Heading for the exit, the silver-empanelled 19th-century Rajasthan furniture is extraordinary, especially the howdah with its stylised silver tigers. In the Renaissance Treasury, pause to look at the German silver partridge and hawk of c 1600. Finally to the giftshop which, with goods priced from 50 pence to £3300, is evidently catering for a range of customers.

At this end of the Somerset House complex, there are a number of rooms open to the public free of charge. Of these, the King's Barge House in the basement is a bit of a letdown, while the best is the Seamen's Waiting Hall, a quite lovely Palladian lobby connecting the courtyard with the Terrace. There is also an agreeable smoky bar, a very reasonably priced café, the pricey Admiralty restaurant, and a stylish, simple summer terrace restaurant, rather expensive for what it is, but a lovely place to sit out on a fine day, looking out over the river, and trying to ignore the fumes and noise of the traffic on the Embankment below.

Hunterian Museum

ADDRESS Royal College of
Surgeons of England,
35–43 Lincoln's Inn Fields,
London WC2A 3PN
(020 7312 2190;
museums@rcseng.ac.uk)
WEBSITE www.rcseng.ac.uk

OPEN Monday to Friday,
10.00–17.00. Closed bank
holidays
ADMISSION free
GETTING THERE underground to
Holborn or Temple

The Museums of the Royal College of Surgeons comprise the Hunterian, Odontology, Anatomy, and Pathology. However, the Anatomy and Pathology Museums are open only to scholars by arrangement, and so are not included here. The present imposing façade of the Royal College of Surgeons looks out over Lincoln's Inn Fields and covers a reasonably successful post-war agglomeration of the Charles Barry building of 1835, other 19th-century extensions and rebuilds and the replacement of the large portions of the building that were bombed in the war (including the Hunterian gallery). This collection is the surviving part of that bought by the nation from John Hunter (some two thirds having been lost in the bombing). The more extensive Hunterian Museum at the University of Glasgow is formed around the collection of John's eldest brother William. Surgery and collecting thus seems to have run in the family.

The slightly forbidding entrance to the Royal College of Surgeons is staffed by approachable people who seem happy to direct visitors to the museum on the first floor. Once there, the post-war barrel-vaulted gallery is a pleasant enough space, in which glass cases abound – and remembering to turn the lights on and off on each case begins to be something of a trial. The stock in trade comprises natural-history specimens with the emphasis on the human being as subject. While there are fascinating skeletons of, for example, the dodo or the spitting cobra or the Irish giant of the 18th century, the more stomach-churning experience is to be derived from the many exhibits displayed in jars of formaldehyde or other preservative. Much of this material will be of greater interest to the specialist than to the layperson, but there is some fascinating stuff. Did you know, for example, that the stomach protects itself from its own acids by the production of antibodies, which cease to be produced after death, whereupon the stomach digests itself? Fascinating, eh?

Some of the pathology specimens, of which there are an enormous number, are quite hard to take: tumorous tissue, and necrotic and syphilitic bone samples and so on. Other material has the strangest beauty about it – there are numerous casts of arterial systems, all of which form magnificent artworks. In something of the same vein, the collection of human foetuses starts off as being worrying, but the potential for horror is rapidly outweighed by the poignancy of these exhibits. Note especially the quintuplets, now more than 200 years old (though many of the other foetuses are post-war). The real, deliberate art is largely unheralded and includes some worthwhile stuff. I particularly like Stubbs' *Rhinoceros* and *Yak*.

Upstairs, the gallery has a great many more specimens in jars, of which by this time most people will be tiring. Also there is the Lister collection of surgical instruments, a haunting reminder of just how ghastly it must have been to be ill a century or so ago.

The fact that this is a museum more visited by people with a professional interest than by members of the general public makes for a distinctly old-fashioned feel to the place. Concessions are not made to the latest developments in museum theory. Labelling is severe, and working through the catalogues for each case is hard work. The publications available to buy are limited, and there is a general sense that this a place for the serious-minded.

London Transport Museum

ADDRESS Covent Garden Piazza, London WC2E 7BB (020 7836 8557/020 7379 6344) WEBSITE www.ltmuseum.co.uk OPEN Saturday to Thursday, 10.00–18.00; Friday, 11.00– 18.00. Closed 24–26 December ADMISSION £5.50, concessions £2.95, under-5s free GETTING THERE underground to Covent Garden, Leicester Square or Holborn. Buses to Aldwych

This museum is largely devoted to the history of the entity called London Transport, so it makes no attempt to provide a comprehensive view of the history of transport in general. But for those of us who are keen on public transport in London, it is wonderful. The museum also makes every effort to engage the attention of children, with considerable success.

On the ground floor, the stars of the show are the dozen buses and trams from 1875 to the 1960s. Each vehicle has a dedicated video display, with an occasionally temperamental touch-screen control. You can get on to nearly all of the vehicles, and there are people role-playing conductors or cleaners from the 1920s/1930s on a couple of them. If you want to see (many) more buses and trams, it is possible to arrange a guided visit to London Transport's Acton Depot via the museum. Nostalgic people like me will be moved almost to tears by the storyboards and video devoted to the demise of the trams, and to rage by the continuing phasing out of the Routemaster buses. (The museum wears its heart on its sleeve to some degree.) The other completely captivating installations are the simulated underground-train controls – guaranteed to make you think twice before cursing the driver when the train doesn't pull up exactly where you want it to in future. There are also fascinating installations devoted to the digging of underground tunnels, with photographs, models, and full-scale tableaux, and a wonderful

storyboard on the Green Line buses, including great photographs from the 1920s and 1930s. Note particularly the photographs of the wonderful Poland Street coach station, which was opened in 1930 and then closed in 1933 because of the congestion it was creating. Less successful on this floor are some of the interactive installations devoted to ticketing and flow control: they are insufficiently labelled, and their purpose is not clear.

Upstairs on the mezzanine floor is a temporary exhibition space, bizarrely devoted to Thomas the Tank Engine at the time of writing. On the top floor there is an excellent storyboard installation on the history of London buses, together with a video whose entertainment format vitiates its impact. A modern bus is there, for people to try sitting in the driver's seat. Less effective is the Fast Forward exhibition, a high-tech installation marred by too much clutter and noise, and, at the time of writing, with more than half of the interactive stuff not in working order. Also up here is part of a steam-hauled underground train, with a locomotive and carriages that you can go into.

Back downstairs, the museum shop has a fine selection of toys and models, and a modest selection of books.

Overall, there is a vitality about this museum, perhaps because it is devoted to such an important and involving aspect of London life. It is small, but of great political and social importance. Admission ought to be free – and probably compulsory.

National Gallery

ADDRESS Trafalgar Square,
London WC2N 5DN
(020 7747 2885;
information@ng-london.org.uk)
WEBSITE www.nationalgallery.
org.uk
OPEN daily 10.00–18.00
(Wednesday until 21.00). Closed
24–26 December, 1 January,
Good Friday.
ADMISSION free
GETTING THERE underground
to Leicester Square or Charing
Cross. Buses 24, 29 to Trafalgar
Square

The National Gallery houses Britain's principal collection of (mainly) European paintings from the period 1260–1900. For those of us who live in London, any attempt to look round the whole of the National Gallery in one go is a) crazy, but b) a reminder of just how many old favourites are housed here – a bit like rediscovering that *Hamlet* is full of quotes. But if you have no choice but to attempt the place in one or two visits, then the gallery has devised a number of ways to make it as rewarding and worthwhile as possible. First of all, the gallery floorplan and signage divides the collection up into four periods: 1260–1510, 1510–1600, 1600–1700, and 1700–1900, any one of which would make a reasonable day's expedition. If your interests lie more in the 20th century, then you're in the wrong place, try the Tate Modern instead. The National also provides in the Microgallery a wonderful computer database with information on every picture in the gallery, using which you can more or less work out what you most want to see. Free audio material is also available, so that, having found an intriguing painting, you can get background information on it then and there. This is one of the most remarkable art collections in the world: what follows is just a quick tour, taking in some of the most famous paintings, as well as my own favourites.

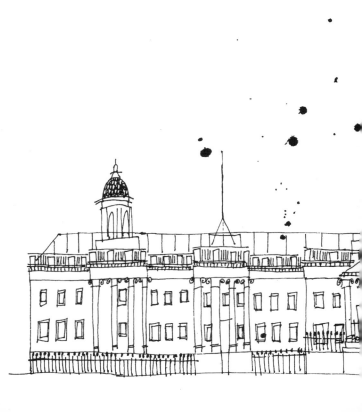

Start at the entrance to the Sainsbury Wing, at the north-west corner of Trafalgar Square: a pleasant enough if unexciting building designed by Venturi, Scott-Brown and Associates, and opened in 1991. Supermarket profits saved the extension from the Thatcherite ethos which would have demanded that development of the site be primarily geared towards offices, with the gallery extension stuck on top. The basics – cloakroom, lavatories, shop are all here to be taken advantage of at the beginning and/or end of your visit. The basement of the Sainsbury Wing is where the main special exhibitions take place, and on the first floor is the agreeable brasserie, with its superb Paula Rego mural. This is a nice place for lunch, although not particularly cheap, but it gets booked up so it's worth phoning ahead for a table.

On the second floor is the collection of paintings from 1260 to 1510. The paintings are splendidly hung in a series of largely top-lit galleries with pale grey walls and (increasingly rather grimy) blonde wood floors. The collection of Italian old masters includes works by Leonardo da Vinci, Duccio, Raphael, etc. After a while, all the virgins, all the children, all the legendary status of the artists begins to get a bit much, and there is a risk of things disappearing in an exotic blur. But focus momentarily for Mantegna's amazing *Introduction of the Cult of Cybele at Rome* in room 61, and the Wilton Diptych in Room 53, whose extraordinary array of blue and white angel wings still, in its poignant gaiety, shouts out across the centuries. The Flemish and Dutch paintings include some wonderful portraits, not least van Eyck's celebrated – and to my mind libellous – *Arnolfini Portrait* in room 56, apparently depicting prenuptial bliss between the severe-looking Signor Arnolfini and his heavily-pregnant fiancée. However, 'the woman's apparently swollen form does not imply pregnancy', we are reassured by the accompanying wallcard. Also not to be missed is Bartolomé Bermejo's dream-like *Saint Michael triumphant over the Devil with the Donor Antonio Juan* in room 64 – Hieronymus Bosch meets Millais.

Passing through to the West Wing where the 1510–1600 collection is housed takes you into the William Wilkins main building completed in 1838, pleasing in its 19th-century way, with glass roofs, ornate marble and gilt, painted plasterwork and figured green and red wallcoverings, which provide a surprisingly effective background for the paintings. There are Venetians such as Veronese, Titian and Tintoretto in room 9, and Florentines including Michelangelo and Bronzino in room 8. Bronzino's *Portrait of a Young Man* is particularly striking here. Moving on, my own favourites are El Greco's *Agony in the Garden of Gethsemane* in room 7, and Cranach's hilarious *Cupid Complaining to Venus* in room 4. You may also wish to see the original of Quinten Massys' overhyped *Grotesque Old Woman* in room 12.

In the 1600–1700 section of the gallery, there is such a profusion of famous works that it is hard to describe: bucketloads of Poussins, stacks of Rembrandts, many of them familiar from reproductions so entrenched in the consciousness that their presence feels atavistic, Rubens by the roomful, and endless Dutch church interiors and sleepy landscapes, with the occasional absolutely arresting Ruisdael or Hobbema among them. My favourites of the period include van Hoogstraten's intriguing peepshow off room 17 and Champaigne's composite portrait of Richelieu in room 18. Moving on from these, in room 30 there are some remarkable Spanish paintings, among which one probably ought to at least glance at Velásquez' *The Toilet of Venus* (the Rokeby Venus), and Murillo's irresistible if rather kitsch *Peasant Boy Leaning on a Sill*. The Caravaggios in room 32 are also remarkable, especially his *Supper at Emmaeus* and his extraordinary, ugly *Boy Bitten by a Lizard*, inexplicably celebrated in some quarters for its – to my mind invisible – paedoeroticism.

The 1700–1900 section of the gallery seems to me to work less well than it should. Too many 18th-century ladies in gay hats with their male counterparts looking smug in powdered wigs, perhaps, and at the other end of the chronology maybe too many undifferentiable Monets. Having said that, there are some striking individual pictures. Turner's two most famous works – *Rain, Steam and Speed* and *The Fighting Temeraire tugged to her Last Berth to be broken up* – are both here in room 34, which is a relief if you have been to the Tate and missed them. And Turner's boldness, his avant-garde once-in-a-century genius presence, hits you straight between the eyes when these are hung in this company. Another revelatory painting is Stubbs' *Whistle-jacket*: for those of us who usually register 19th-century animal paintings just long enough to shield our eyes, this is something else.

There is a decent enough café in the basement of the main building, quite well run, and large enough usually to avoid overcrowding, although it can be pretty busy at lunchtimes. The other thing to check before leaving the main building is whether there is a special exhibition off the main vestibule. The regular free exhibitions held here are small-scale jewels, enabling a new perspective on often-familiar artists or works. Recent examples have included 'Recognising van Eyck' in 1998, when a very few of van Eyck's most famous works were brought together from around the world, and 'Henry Moore and the National Gallery', when some bronze maquettes of Moore's were put on show beside the works from the National Gallery's collection which had inspired them.

Returning to the Sainsbury Wing, the main museum shop is a prince among such institutions – a large agreeable space with lots of good reproductions from the gallery's collections, and a serious range of art-history books. Even the tat's just about worth looking at.

National Portrait Gallery

ADDRESS St Martin's Place,
London WC2H 0HE
(020 7312 2463)
WEBSITE www.npg.org.uk
OPEN Monday to Wednesday,
Saturday, Sunday, 10.00–18.00;
Thursday, Friday, 10.00–21.00
ADMISSION free
GETTING THERE underground
to Leicester Square,
Embankment or Charing Cross.
Bus 24 or 29

The magnificent Victorian bulk of the National Portrait Gallery is doomed forever to reside in the shadow of its neighbour, the National Gallery. One of the great advantages of this is that the Portrait Gallery is usually uncrowded. However, more attention has been paid to it since the opening in May 2000 of the new Ondaatje Wing, filling in a small unused space between the backs of the National and the National Portrait Galleries. The new wing, designed by Jeremy Dixon and Edward Jones, is an attractive space that has served to bring something of a new lease of life to the gallery as a whole.

It is all too easy to give in to the temptation to get no further than the contemporary, special exhibition, and photographic galleries on the ground floor, also checking out the late-20th-century worthies in the new Balcony Gallery on the first floor. There is no doubt that pictures of one's personal heroes and villains from the present day exert a great fascination, but we seem as a nation to display a depressing absence of playfulness. There are some exceptions, of course, of which my own favourite is Hans Schwarz's 1984 *Trade Union Leaders* in which three men caricatured time and again in the press as something between the devil incarnate and a joke of attitudinised solemnity and mundanity – Joe Gormley, Tom Jackson and Sid Weighell – are transformed into something camply spectacular, in perhaps a moment of real insight into the nature of the men within. This painting's new siting in the Balcony Gallery does not do it full justice, but it is still remarkable.

If you are interested in a particular period, artist or sitter, then either ask the helpful staff at the information desk or walk up to the ground/first floor mezzanine IT gallery, where you can consult the on-line catalogue. Like many such things, the operation of this is pretty counter-intuitive, but practice and help from the counter staff will get you there in the end. For a general tour, take the escalator (the longest above-ground escalator in Europe, allegedly, though this is an unimpressive fact if you've just arrived by tube) past light blank walls to the second floor. Then take the stairs up to the Portrait Restaurant, an elongated space from whose windows there is visible a fantastic central London roofscape. The restaurant interior is a smart ensemble of black and shades of grey, with an agreeable bar and fairly expensive lunch and tea menus. One small portion of the space has been cordoned off as a viewing gallery.

Down again to the Tudor Galleries, with Queen Elizabeth and her contemporaries white-faced, contemplative and unhealthy, standing out from their dark backgrounds, framed in black and gold against the even darker wall colour. Two things to notice especially here are: first, William Sarot's extraordinary skewed-perspective 1546 portrait of Edward VI; second, beside John Taylor's c. 1610 portrait of Shakespeare is a tiny alcove with its window providing a marvellous surreal vista over the escalator and stairs.

Moving on to the 17th- and 18th-century paintings, these begin chronologically with mainly monarchs idealised in vision – not always to good effect. The 18th-century portraits mark the high point of the genre. In room 12, Reynolds' c. 1756 portrait of Samuel Johnson, and Gainsborough's startlingly modern-looking J C Bach of about 1776 are extraordinary, as are Reynolds' c. 1749 self-portrait and his 1760 Laurence Sterne. One flaw of the 17th- and 18th-century portraits is that they nearly all make the sitters look astonishingly youthful, as witness Louis Gabriel Blanchot's 1738 portrait of Bonnie Prince Charlie in room 4, which makes the 17-year-old prince look about six. A welcome exception is in room 7, the c. 1680 portrait of Charles II attributed to Thomas Hawker, in which an energetic life seems to have left its mark: how could one fail to like Charles so much better than any of his successors?

A small selection of the drawings collection is usually exhibited in room 16 on a revolving basis, but the collection is so large and the room so small that it really is a tiny sample. In room 17, Karl Anton Hickel's 1793–95 painting *France Declares War on England: Pitt addresses the House of Commons*, brings together in one huge canvas a group portrait of many of the leading figures of the day. Unfortunately, while the key provided helpfully identifies some celebrated – Fox, Sheridan – and less-celebrated – Welbore Ellis, who he? – figures, it leaves an awful lot of fascinating faces unidentified. There seems to have been something of a fashion from this period on into the middle of the 19th century for large group portraits, but most of them don't work as well as this one does – too much composition, not enough portraiture. Room 18 is devoted to the Romantics, and notable among the paintings here are John Linnell's 1838 portrait of Turner, Alexander Nasmyth's endearing 1787 portrait of Burns, and William Hilton's 1820 John Clare, with incipient madness leaping from the canvas.

Moving on to room 20, this is remarkable in its own right as a Regency display gallery, with green walls, green carpet and green leather bench. There is an overwhelming number of paintings on the walls, hung too close together for there to be any possibility to take them in adequately. The gallery is largely dependent on natural light from above, though with the paintings themselves being spotlit, so that the centre of the room is marooned in gloom, unless the sun is shining. Incidentally, don't miss the miniatures, which are in glass cases shielded with leather drapes at one end of the room: they are superb, the best things in this room, and include the famous portrait of Jane Austen by her sister Cassandra.

Down on the first floor, there is the bulk of the 19th century to be tackled. In room 21 a formidable array of dusty black busts occupies one end of the room, outstaring the viewer with ease. There is also Henry Jamyn Brooks' amazing *Private View of the Old Masters Exhibition, Royal Academy, 1888* with a key to who's who, including G F Watts, Frederick Leighton, and Lawrence Alma-Tadema, leching after an unidentified woman, while Lady Alma-Tadema looks on disapprovingly from a short distance away. Other remarkable works on this floor include Branwell Brontë's c. 1834 portrait of his rather daunting sisters in room 24, while room 26 is the only room in the gallery devoted to the work of a single painter – G F Watts. In room 29, William Orpen's work quite leaps off the wall. His 1900 portrait of Augustus John is terrific, and his 1909 *The Selecting Jury of the New English Art Club* is both a wonderful portrait and a great painting, with an early cubist influence apparent. In the same room, I find my expectations utterly confounded by John Singer Sargent's 1894 portrait of

Coventry Patmore. Across in room 27, the Victorian photographs of scientists are not to be missed, and include some familiar images, such as Robert Howlett's 1857 photograph of Brunel standing in front of enormous chains. Less familiar, but utterly compelling, is Julia Margaret Cameron's 1867 picture of Sir John Herschel.

There are also some great photographs in the central showcases of room 31, the large gallery on this floor. And as we move into the middle of the 20th century in this room, a curious ambivalence starts to make itself felt in the painted portraits. Augustus John's 1937/38 portrait of Dylan Thomas, for example, seems simultaneously compellingly attractive and quite repulsive, while Feliks Topolski's extraordinary 1943 portrait of H G Wells seems to show the old man genial and despairing by turns.

The Britain 1960–90 collection in the Balcony Gallery is in many ways fascinating. There is, however, a significant conservatism in the style of many of the portraits on show, combined with tremendous toadyism in some cases. Overall, the modern pictures are problematic in a number of ways. There is a tendency to have each subject represented once and once only, regardless of who executed the portrait. And I find myself unavoidably far more interested in the matter of who is being painted rather than the qualities of the painting, or who painted it. In short, one tends to look at the label first, and then the painting, in a reversal of more usual practice. (Having said which, throughout the National Portrait Gallery the little potted biographies of the subjects given on the labels are well-judged and fascinating.) This gallery is dominated by photographs of Isaiah Berlin and Margaret Thatcher by Richard Avedon and Helmut Newton respectively, perhaps reflecting the polarities of late-20th-century

Britain. More fun is the wonderful 1985 painting of Dorothy Hodgkin by Maggi Hambling.

On the stairway and the first part of the ground floor display, there are far too many witless royal portraits. However, in room 39 on the ground floor there are some fascinating photographs of the people responsible for the gallery's recent extension – builders, trustees, staff, and donors – quite a cross-section of British society. Elsewhere on this floor are some compelling photographs of contemporary icons. It is currently all too easy to miss the basement, with its truly excellent bookshop, distinct from the shop on the ground floor, and attractive though quite expensive café, where you sit under glass between the front wall of the gallery and the Charing Cross Road.

Odontological Museum

ADDRESS Royal College of
Surgeons of England,
35–43 Lincoln's Inn Fields,
London WC2A 3PN (020 7312
2190; museums@rcseng.ac.uk)
WEBSITE www.rcseng.ac.uk

OPEN Mondays to Fridays,
10.00–17.00. Closed bank
holidays
ADMISSION free
GETTING THERE underground to
Holborn or Temple

Technically, this is a separate entity from the Hunterian within the Royal College of Surgeons. In fact, it forms an annexe to the Hunterian, through which the most obvious entry to the Odontological Museum lies. Once there, it is a large chilly room, all too reminiscent of that in which much of my childhood dentistry took place, only bigger. For anybody with West-of-Scotland teeth, this is a terrifying place. Although there is a comprehensive collection of primate jaws, soothing in their mere savagery, the human jaw and tooth sections are simply too distressing to discuss, as are the dental instruments through the ages. Most instructive, however, to note that an implement identical to one used on me in the 1970s is said to have fallen into desuetude around 1850.

Overall, this is old-fashioned, glass-case stuff, really not very accessible to the lay person. The one attempt to put in place a more up-to-date approach is embodied in the 'So You Think You Know Your Anatomy' exhibit – a series of photographs of jaw sections with numbered components, and concealed peek-a-boo answers to the side – but the subject-matter is clearly aimed at second-year-and-above dental students.

There is some quite interesting stuff on the use of dental evidence in dating archaeological digs, and some surely obsolete evolutionary material. In among all this are some quite horrifying, fascinating but seemingly irrelevant stuff on Cyclopes. And, just when you thought the horror was over, skulls of 6–9 year-olds, just stuffed with teeth.

This is clearly aimed primarily at specialists, who may be able to make head or tail of the drawers and drawers full of tooth and palate samples.

Percival David Foundation of Chinese Art

ADDRESS 53 Gordon Square,
London WC1H OPD
(020 7387 3909)
OPEN Monday to Friday,
10.30–17.00

ADMISSION free
GETTING THERE underground
to Russell Square, Goodge Street
or Euston Square

Technically part of the University of London's School of Oriental and African Studies, this collection of Chinese ceramics is a largely undiscovered gem, situated just off the southern end of Gordon Square. You are likely to have the place pretty well to yourself, and the quality of the display is outstanding.

On the ground floor, the first room that you enter is an exercise in institutional minimalism, with white cabinets against white walls. The relatively sparsely populated display cases impart a serene feeling of importance to each piece. The monochrome Ming pieces from the 15th and 16th centuries glow with colour, and are simply wonderful. In the second ground-floor room, an even stronger sense of simple exquisite beauty adheres to the cloudy, grey-green Song Dynasty Ru and Jun ware, the former being of exceptional rarity and of particular interest to the specialist.

Upstairs on the first floor, the two rooms are less effectively minimalist than the ground-floor displays, but still with that serenity of the Song monochrome pieces. More of the Ru pieces, and also some cream-coloured Ding ware of the 11th century. These have wonderful fluid shapes, with raised patterns, but no additional colour to distract from the ethereal simplicity of the shapes and the cloudy beauty of the glaze.

On the second floor, one is initially overwhelmed by the sight of more of the familiar blue and white Ming pieces than you could shake a stick at. Here and there among all the blue, the occasional red-underglazed stem-cup or bowl seems transcendently beautiful. Following these, the polychrome pieces both of the 15th/16th century Ming dynasty and the 18th century Qing seem a bit Chinese-restauranty, however fine they may be objectively. Finally, though, in the last room are monochrome white, grey, blue, yellow and red pieces from the Ming and Qing dynasties, dating from the 15th to the 18th centuries. These are riotously, triumphantly colourful, and will send you on your way with a feeling of uplift.

There is also a specialist library for scholars to consult by arrangement.

Petrie Museum of Egyptian Archaeology

ADDRESS University College
London, Malet Place, London
WC1E 6BT (020 7679 2884;
petrie.museum@ucl.ac.uk)
OPEN Tuesday to Friday,
13.00–17.00; Saturday,

10.00–13.00
ADMISSION free
GETTING THERE underground to
Russell Square, Goodge Street,
Euston Square

Like the Percival David Foundation, this is one of the University of London's hidden treasures, this time housed within one of University College's buildings. Unlike the Percival David Foundation, however, there is nothing serenely minimalist about the case upon case of crowded artefacts dating from pre-dynastic times through to the Roman occupation of Egypt. The sheer quantity of stuff is overwhelming, and there is any amount more in drawers awaiting cataloguing. Also, few concessions are made to the non-specialist – small typed labels provide details of the scholarly publication in which details of each piece can be found, with only a small minority marked 'unpublished', and through open doors curatorial discussions can be heard, and strange conservatorial activities dimly described.

In the first room that one comes into, there are cases of pots, the significance of which can surely only be apparent to professionals. Among all this, however, there are pre-dynastic (say, 4th millennium BCE) decorated earthenware pieces, whose sheer antiquity makes the mind reel, and among which the Naqada pieces in particular are genuinely beautiful. Also in this first room there is a table-case with some fascinating examples of Egyptian writing of various dynasties. Perhaps the most moving exhibits in this room are the linen dresses, two or three from the 5th dynasty (2494–2345 BCE), and one, the Tarkhan Dress which 'can

lay claim to being the earliest garment in the world', by which they obviously mean surviving garment. This is from the 1st dynasty (3100–2890 BCE), and although much damaged, it is still very much there, a linen dress with a ruched top, just 5000 years older than one might have expected a dress to be. There is also an extraordinary beaded dress, very stylish, the epitome of flapperdom in the 1920s, except that this one dates from 2400 BCE.

In the second room, there are cases of carved stelae, some of them painted, with familiar-looking hieroglyphics and stylised portraits, and also a considerable number of those wonderful Egyptian cats, and other stylised animals. Many of these are from Hierakonpolis, and date from the early 3rd millennium BCE. The thing about these familiar-looking pieces is partly that so many survive at all, and then that so many survive here. A staircase leads down off to a fire exit at one side of the room, and this, too, is lined with cabinets full of stuff. But it cannot be ignored. There are model boats, variously from the pre-dynastic era through to the 1st intermediate period, and they are remarkable.

Among the many, many other objects worth looking at, those which most attracted my attention included the set of 18th dynasty opium measures, and the speaking likenesses from the time of the Roman occupation, painted on wood panels, and familiar from reproductions elsewhere. But these are the originals.

Oh, and there's the odd richly painted wooden mummy case or coffin lid lying casually around …

Pollock's Toy Museum

ADDRESS 1 Scala Street, London
W1P 1LT (020 7636 3452;
toymuseum@hotmail.com)
WEBSITE www.pollocks.cwc.net
OPEN 10.00–17.00 except
Sunday and bank holidays
ADMISSION £3.00, under-18s
£1.50
GETTING THERE underground to
Goodge Street

This toy collection is disposed through six small cluttered rooms in two adjoining houses, one dating from the late 18th century, the other from the late 19th. From its publicity material, it is clear that the museum's self-image is as a place which children will enjoy visiting – and so they may. However, it is anything but hands-on in its approach: many of the exhibits are old and delicate (valuable too, I would imagine), and so virtually all are housed in glass cases. Labelling is exiguous, but the helpful free guide to the museum compensates for this. Because of the steep narrow stairs and small crowded rooms, there is a one-way system in operation from which it would be awkward and antisocial to deviate. Generally, this place has strong overtones of Angela Carter, and will probably appeal most to those with a taste for the gothic.

Highlights for me include the Edwardian 'boy's den' in room 1 and 'girl's nursery' in room 5, which just need a waxwork boy or girl to complete the sense of an offbeat and unsettling presence. The collection of model locomotives in room 1 is great, as are the tinplate model cars from the 1920s and 1930s in room 2. Eric in room 4 is claimed as 'the oldest known teddy bear', though I wonder if this can be right, since there is a bear from the same year in the Bethnal Green Museum (see page 177), with no similar claim being made for it. As well as Eric's ursine companions from 1905 to the 1970s, there are several mid-19th-century dolls' houses in this room, and a lovely model shop. There is a large collection of dolls in rooms 3 and 5, from the early 19th century onwards, together with some super toy kitchens and horses and carts.

On the stairs down, the collection of war-time toys includes a game 'War in the Falklands', made in the USA and banned in Britain after a few weeks of sales, on the extraordinary grounds of 'poor taste'.

Downstairs again to room 6, which not only houses a splendid collection of toy theatres but also a tableau of a shop selling toy theatres. Perhaps this is intended as a hint for when you make your way back down to the ground floor, and the rather wonderful functioning old-fashioned toyshop. Like the museum, though, the shop feels more like the kind of place which adults like and self-consciously declare to be thrilling for children, rather than the sort of place that children themselves actually enjoy all that much.

Sir John Soane's Museum

ADDRESS 13 Lincoln's Inn Fields, London WC2 (020 7405 2107) OPEN Tuesday to Saturday, 10.00–17.00

ADMISSION free
GETTING THERE underground to Holborn

This is a superbly unorthodox place in every way, perhaps taking its cue, in part, from John Soane's own life. Soane (1753–1837) was an architectural genius, a collector of antiquities, a wealthy man, and, it would seem, an absolutely ghastly parody of the genial and reliable paterfamilias. But Soane's personal strangeness seems to be reflected and enlarged in these three town houses which he acquired both as home for himself and his family and as a setting for his collection of *objets d'art*. Having filled the three buildings with his collection of wonders, he then apparently devoted his considerable energies to making the whole affair as strange as possible.

Entrance is free, but, having rung the doorbell and been admitted by slightly fierce staff who will then make you sign the visitors' book, you may feel that the nervous energy expended in getting thus far has been considerable. Don't worry, you ain't seen nothin' yet. The great thing in this museum is not to trust first impressions: they will invariably be wrong, having been misled by Soane's devotion to *trompe l'oeil* techniques of various sorts. Whatever you think is a door will be a mirror, a mirror a window, and a window, well, something else. Do not miss the hinged gallery, in which a series of folding panels provides about six times as much hanging space as would be available otherwise.

Unfortunately, the *trompe l'oeil* habit here extends to other faculties, as the hugely informative spiel given by the men who, er, give the spiel has been observed to contain some half-truths or even downright lies. Best of all for me was when a considerable time was devoted to one obscure work by some incredibly obscure 18th-century print-maker, and no mention made of the fact that Hogarth's *Rake's Progress* on the wall is the original.

Because of the layout of the basement galleries, it is quite difficult at times to work out whether you are inside the main building or not, and this disorientation effect is reinforced by the extraordinary collection of real and fake statuary, all of it displayed hugger-mugger to remarkable sculptural effect. That is to say that the arrangement of the basement exhibits itself could qualify as a sort of installation-art, of a high order. A curious bathos is provided here by the bath-shaped sarcophagus, an unexpectedly domestic note in what is otherwise a fine collection of the weird.

Throughout the building, it is rewarding to look up from time to time, to note the extraordinary ceiling shapes, which are various and eye-catching, with the recurring curved motif pinched from Soane by Giles Gilbert Scott for the familiar telephone-box design. On the ground floor, the breakfast parlour is not only a beautiful room in its own right, but also provides a misleading air of normality in this strange house. To the front of the breakfast parlour is the exhibition room, which seems to contrive to host a series of temporary exhibitions of a level of banality extraordinary by any standards, but the more so in this highly original setting. Upstairs on the first floor, the drawing room is absolutely magnificent, a reminder if one were needed that the way in which houses were decorated around 1800 was far from stuffy or austere.

Altogether an odd establishment, and with a capacity to wrongfoot the visitor such that one is likely to emerge gasping for a drink. Unfortunately there is no café in the museum, and only the rather unsatisfactory open-air affair in the middle of Lincoln's Inn Fields immediately to hand. But there are pubs round the corner on Holborn, not all of them poisonous.

Theatre Museum

ADDRESS Russell Street, London
WC2E 7PA (020 7836 7891)
OPEN Tuesday to Sunday,
10.00–18.00. Closed public
holidays
ADMISSION £4.50, unemployed
and students £2.50, under-16s
and over-60s free
GETTING THERE underground to
Holborn, Leicester Square or
Covent Garden. Buses to
Aldwych

Your first encounter with the Theatre Museum involves the ground-floor exhibition space, which houses temporary exhibitions, usually comprising interactive material particularly attractive to children (though adults can be seen queuing behind 8-year-olds for the chance to try their hand at manipulating a giant ghoul). Moving downstairs past a series of photographs from historic theatrical productions takes you to an extensive sample from the National Video Archive of Stage Performance, which takes place in a viewing room accommodating perhaps 25 people.

The main gallery is devoted to a chronological sequence of set models from Shakespearean theatre through to the present day, augmented by props, paintings and video. There are then a couple of semi-permanent exhibitions, one devoted to *The Wind In the Willows*, with irresistible video footage from rehearsals of the National Theatre production. The Irving Gallery contains a semi-permanent exhibition devoted to stage design, with the emphasis on the innovative and wonderful early 20th-century set designs of Edward Gordon Craig. There is also a full-scale theatre foyer used as an exhibition space for pictures of actors in celebrated roles over the years. This is mainly oriented towards children or to people with a specific interest in the technical aspects of mounting a production. The extensive archive material is accessible to scholars by arrangement.

Wallace Collection

ADDRESS Hertford House,
Manchester Square, London
WIM 6BN (020 7563 9500)
WEBSITE www.wallace-
collection.org.uk
OPEN Monday to Saturday,
10.00–17.00; Sunday,
12.00–17.00. Closed 24–26
December, 1 January, Good
Friday, May Day bank holiday
ADMISSION free
GETTING THERE underground
to Bond Street. Buses along
Oxford Street

Though only a short walk away from Oxford Street and Bond Street, and despite the renowned masterpieces among its pictures, the Wallace Collection remains a remarkably undervisited place. Hertford House is an agreeable 18th-century town house, which belonged to the Marquesses of Hertford. The eponymous Wallace was Sir Richard, illegitimate son of the fourth Marquess, and it was Sir Richard's widow who in 1897 left the collection to the nation on the condition that it always be housed in central London. The recent extension of the building by Rick Mather has provided basement gallery space and a restaurant in the attractive glass-roofed central courtyard – nice space, nice menu, but hopelessly disorganised when I was last there.

Unless you have a special interest in armour or in Sèvres porcelain, then the pictures are the main point here. Start in the Great Gallery on the first floor, where Frans Hals' *Laughing Cavalier* greets you at eye-level and as close quarters as you could wish, a reassuringly human presence. If that is too familiar, move on to the wonderful 'studio of Rembrandt' double double portraits hung further along the same wall – Susanna van Collen and daughter, and her husband Jean Pellicorne and son. Now look at the Van Dyck portraits hung opposite – Philippe le Roy and Marie de Raet. Not only is the symmetry of the double double por-

trait hanging maintained, but there is a pointed parallel between the children of one set and the dogs of the other. (Not to mention the old maxim about people coming to look like their dogs, further reinforced by Gainsborough's magnificent *Mrs Robinson* [*Perdita*] on the west wall.) Among the many other super paintings in this room are works by Rembrandt, Titian, Murillo and Velásquez, as well as two less-well-known paintings which are great favourites of mine: Philippe de Champaigne's portrait *An Echevin of Paris*, and Salvator Rosa's *River Landscape with Apollo and the Cumaean Sibyl*, surely the very essence of proto-romanticism. The hanging is one of the most successful double-decker arrangements that I know, though connoisseurs of dead-animal paintings may disagree.

Elsewhere in the collection, the East Galleries are largely devoted to 17th-century Dutch and Flemish works, among which Rubens' startling *Adoration of the Magi* demonstrates what a camel in a good mood would look like. A very different note is struck by Gerrit Dou's haunting *Hermit* in the same room, while Jan Steen's lively demotic *Celebrating the Birth* (1664) and *Merry-making in a Tavern* are splendidly cheery. There are also a couple of wonderful de Hooch interiors and some fine Hobbema landscapes. Moving round to The Boudoir, Reynolds' *St John in the Wilderness* is a strange, worrying depiction of what seems to be a 1920s chorus for boy and lamb. In the West Galleries, the 18th-century French painting is largely unexciting, though shining out are Fragonard's *A Young Scholar* and his joyously sexy *The Swing*. Nothing shines from the unspeakably dreary 19th-century stuff.

The ground floor is a mixed bag. There is lots and lots of European and Oriental armour, some of it visually arresting,

like the late-14th-century Bascinet in European Armoury 1, or the remarkable Ashanti stuff in the middle of the Oriental Armoury. (That's oriental in the Edward Said sense, I take it.) Elsewhere there is a considerable amount of Sèvres and early majolica ware, while the 16th-century gallery has a range of material, including glassware, and small bronzes. Of particular note here is Carlo Crivelli's astonishing etiolated portrait of St Roch.

The new basement rooms comprise a library (open by appointment), education suite, and temporary exhibition space; also a watercolour gallery with a revolving display, a conservation gallery, and a display of material from the reserve collection, some of which is second-rate or of dubious provenance, and some of which is fine.

north london

Estorick Collection

ADDRESS 39a Canonbury Square, London N1 2AN (020 7704 9522)
OPEN Wednesday to Saturday, 11.00–18.00; Sunday, 12.00–17.00. Closed 25 December to 1 January, and some days at Easter – phone to check
ADMISSION £3.50, concessions £2.50
GETTING THERE underground to Highbury & Islington, then walk (5 minutes)

There is something rather wonderful about a collection as specialised as this, having its residence in an admittedly absolutely beautiful house, but distinctly off the beaten track as far as museums are concerned. The Estorick Collection is devoted entirely to 20th-century Italian art, and contains some fine works by Modigliani, de Chirico, and Morandi, and some of the futurist followers of Marinetti. However, some of the permanent collection display – particularly the drawings – is rotated quite regularly, so what you see on your visit may be a matter of the luck of the draw, so to speak.

The downstairs gallery space is usually devoted to temporary exhibitions, with the permanent collection displayed upstairs. Don't miss Balla's extraordinary 'Hand of the Violinist' in gallery 3, nor, for example, Boccioni's *Dynamism of a Cyclist* among the impressive collection of drawings in gallery 6.

There is a reasonable café on the ground floor, and a small bookshop run by a fierce woman. But the wonderful thing about this place is the beauty of the house and garden.

Fenton House

ADDRESS Windmill Hill, London
NW3 6RT (020 7435 347)
OPEN 1 April to 31 October,
Saturday, Sunday and bank-
holiday Mondays, 11.00–17.00;
Wednesday to Friday,
14.00–17.00

ADMISSION £4.20, no
concessions
GETTING THERE underground to
Hampstead, then note that the
main entrance to the house is
from Hampstead Grove

This agreeable late 17th-century house is tucked away in a back street in Hampstead, and houses a remarkable collection of keyboard instruments as well as some fine porcelain, and unusual 17th-century needlework pictures. The house is run by the National Trust, which shows, rather, in a dedication to preserving a genteel atmosphere at the expense of providing any information on the bulk of the exhibits.

On the ground floor there is a good deal of fine Regency furniture, and a couple of harpsichords, one of them built in 1612, and allegedly used by Handel at one stage in its life. Moving up to the first floor, there is cabinet after cabinet of porcelain, mainly Meissen and Rockingham figurines, but also a great array of second-rate blue and white Qing stuff of the 17th/18th centuries. There are some more keyboard instruments, though the most interesting part of the collection is housed upstairs in the attics. Harpsichords and virginals of the 16th to 18th centuries form the main body of the collection, and many have exceptionally fine painted or inlaid woodwork. This being the National Trust, there is no labelling around and no information is given on any of these in the little printed guide that they have the cheek to charge you for on top of the entrance fee, and none of the volunteers knows much about them. Nevertheless, they are beautiful and interesting to look at.

The gardens here are absolutely magnificent, though marred by the presence of numbers of under-employed Hampstead people, who have worked out that they can bring their offspring to revel in these suitably genteel surroundings without having to pay and with not much chance of encountering the lower orders. There is a splendid walled garden, lawns, an orchard and kitchen garden, with an earnest gardener stirring mulch or compost or whatever.

Freud Museum

ADDRESS 20 Maresfield Gardens, London NW3 5SX (020 7435 2002) OPEN Wednesday to Sunday, 12.00–17.00. Closed Christmas and Easter ADMISSION £4, concessions £2 GETTING THERE underground to Swiss Cottage or Finchley Road, then walk (10 minutes)

The presence of the Freud Museum strikes an odd note among the vulgar glitz of this South Hampstead backwater – the sort of area in which the residents park the Ferrari on the street, reserving the triple garage for the really good cars. Sigmund Freud spent only the last year of his life in London, so it is perhaps to be expected that the museum seems to contain more of the spirit of his daughter Anna than of Freud himself. Upstairs in the Video Room, it is Anna's voice which dominates as she takes us through a series of dogs and camera-toting princesses at what feels like inordinate length. There is also a rather more serious video by Edward Engelman, mainly recording scenes from Freud's life prior to his decampment from Vienna. But this is feeling its age rather: more interesting are the still photographs by Engelman, of which, unfortunately, only a very small selection are on display.

Elsewhere in the house, there is a collection of agreeable Viennese furniture, and a remarkable number of Egyptian and Roman antiquities collected by Freud himself. Although many of these appear to be of museum quality in their own right, the amount of detail given about them on the information cards is limited. Instead, and somewhat disconcertingly, small placards throughout the museum give odd little case histories or otherwise theorise the interpretation of dreams.

It is in his huge gloomy library and study on the ground

floor that Sigmund's personality asserts itself against Anna's. And what a personality. The oppressiveness of the room is accentuated by heavy red curtains, kept closed at all times apparently, and floor-to-ceiling books, the only light relief being from more Egyptian grave-artefacts. The room manages to smell as though somebody had died there recently. Not an attractive advertisement for the teachings of Freud, but fascinating in its capacity for depression. The set-up as it is presented today is as it was established in 1938, and that in turn was designed to reproduce as exactly as possible Freud's library and study in Vienna. The quantity of books and furniture is an indication that however enforced Freud's departure from Vienna may have been, he was no ordinary refugee. But these are no doubt unworthy observations.

After the library, it is worth going to a window overlooking the delightful back garden for a spot of light relief. This is definitely a museum for the serious-minded: indeed, it is the only museum in which I have observed that the majority of the visitors tend to be taking earnest notes, providing an entirely bogus sense of comradeship for the mere frivolous museum-guide writer. Although there is a bookshop, with quite a good selection of Freud (though oddly not every volume of the collected works) and other psychological texts, there is no café and no visible lavatories.

Jewish Museum

ADDRESS Raymond Burton
House, 129–131 Albert Street,
London NW1 7NB
(020 8349 1143)
OPEN Sunday to Thursday,
10.00–16.00, except Jewish
festivals and public holidays
ADMISSION £3, concessions
£1.50
GETTING THERE underground to
Camden Town.
Buses 31, 274, C2

ADDRESS The Sternberg Centre,
80 East End Road, London
N3 2SY (020 7284 1997)
OPEN Monday to Thursday,
10.30–17.00; Sunday,
10.30–16.30, except Jewish
festivals and public holidays.
Closed Sundays in August, bank-
holiday weekends, and 24
December–4 January
ADMISSION variable but typically
£2.00, concessions £1.00
GETTING THERE underground to
Finchley Central, then boring
walk (10–15 minutes)

If ever a split-site institution cried out for unification then
the Jewish Museum is that institution. The distance between
the Camden and the Finchley sites is such that some determination is necessary to embrace both on the same expedition. The faults and virtues of each site reverse those of the
other, however, and a balanced picture of London Jewish
culture is impossible without going to both.

At the Camden Town site, the fairly recent conversion of
the building is smart and professional-looking – the Bond
Street of Jewish cultural display. The keynote is of
respectable and dignified adult museum-going. At the out-
set, a collection of wall-boards promises to set out a history
of the Jews in Britain. Any complacency that the English
might harbour about their lack of anti-semitism is under-
mined fast with the reminder of Edward 1's expulsion of the
Jews in 1290 – but where is the rest of the social history?

(For the answer, see below.) There is on display a collection of more or less impressive portraits and *objets d'art* assembled by the Jewish upper classes in the 18th and 19th centuries: some assertively declaring assimilation, others defensively designed as propitiatory gifts, especially to the Lord Mayor of London, all of them reflecting the condition of the successful but marginalised. A video installation provides an interesting account of Jewish religious festivals and ceremonial, while in the upstairs gallery the display of religious impedimenta – torah scrolls, sabbath lamps, spice boxes or menorahs, for example – would be a silversmith's delight.

A series of respected temporary exhibitions have been mounted in the ground-floor gallery, around two a year on average. There are lavatories in the building, and a number of more or less OK cafés round the corner on Parkway.

It's a bit of a haul out to the Finchley site. When you get there, the museum is forbiddingly sited behind massive security gates. It is in fact a small part of a large Jewish community centre, and the perceived need for such heavy security speaks volumes. The guard on the gate will point you towards the understated museum entrance. Once there, an enthusiastic woman will tell you something of the museum's aspirations. Inside, the museum is very small and unpretentious, occupying a sort of modest-sized, split-level barn. On the ground floor there is a series of installations, mainly relating to working-class Jewish life in London from the 1890s through to the 1950s. The clothing trade, cabinet-making and baking are all covered by these installations, with tools, wall-boards and photographs. The presentation of the material is aimed at children, and lacks a degree of coherence and technical background. It is fascinating, nevertheless.

The main event, however, is the holocaust exhibition upstairs, detailing the life of Leon Greenman, an Auschwitz survivor, who gives talks to schoolchildren and other visitors – almost a living exhibit in his own right, though one of the most engaging museum-pieces that I have ever encountered. Leon attends the museum most Sundays (though beware the opening hours). Since he was a mature adult when he was sent to Auschwitz, his presence at the museum is something to be treasured while it is still possible to do so.

The extraordinary part of the Finchley set-up is the way that the museum caters for school parties. To see quite large groups of schoolchildren – often non-Jewish – completely engaged by Leon Greenman's account of his life is really moving. And Mr Greenman's sensitive and realistic making of connections from the rise of Fascism in the 1930s through to politics or lack of them today is a welcome far cry from some of the holocaust hagiography indulged in by other institutions. Having said that, the presence of school parties in such a small museum space is an awful drawback for the private visitor. So, it would probably be a good idea to telephone the museum before trekking out to Finchley, both to make sure that it is open, and perhaps to make sure that one will avoid any school parties. There is a café and lavatories on site, though not part of the museum itself.

The museum's long-term aspirations are to unite the Camden and Finchley sites, but the amount of money involved in doing this would be very considerable. For the foreseeable future, all that one can say is that each site would do well to attempt to infuse something of the characteristics of the other.

Keats House

ADDRESS Keats Grove, London
NW3 2RR
(020 7435 2062; keatshouse
@corpoflondon.gov.uk)
WEBSITE www.cityoflondon.
gov. uk
OPEN Tuesday to Sunday and
bank-holiday Mondays,
12.00–17.00
ADMISSION £3.00, concessions
£1.50, under-16s free
GETTING THERE underground to
Hampstead or Belsize Park, then
walk (10 minutes)

Unless you have come to worship at the place where 'Ode to a Nightingale' *et al* were written, there is not really very much to see at Keats House beyond an agreeable early-19th-century Hampstead house and garden. There is some original and some replica furniture, and some sketches, prints and paintings of variable quality. Notable are the flower studies in watercolour by Charles Armitage Brown, of around 1836. Also worth seeing are the facsimiles of letters by Keats, the originals of which are available to scholars by arrangement. Otherwise, come on a sunny day and take a stroll in the agreeable garden.

Kenwood House

ADDRESS Hampstead Lane, London NW3 (020 8348 1286) OPEN 1 April to 30 September, daily, 10.00–18.00; October, daily, 10.00–17.00; 1 November to 31 March, daily, 10.00–16.00. Closed 24, 25 December and 1 January ADMISSION free GETTING THERE underground to Hampstead, then walk across Hampstead Heath (c.25 minutes). Or underground to Archway, then 210 bus

With probably the most magnificent setting of any of the places listed in this book, the getting to Kenwood House is almost as important as the arriving, especially if you walk across the Heath from Hampstead underground station. So, before walking round to the entrance (situated at what feels like the rear of the house), pause to look across the sweep of lawns to the lake and the woods beyond. In spring, the flowers and shrubs to the west of the house are absolutely beautiful, and daffodils set off the Henry Moore sculpture in all its brooding profundity. Ahem.

The house is a lovely, tactfully understated neo-classical building, the exterior as it is nowadays visible being by Robert Adam. Although the interior is objectively rather fine, it cannot be said to be shown to best effect as administered at present – the Orangery, for instance, is rather thrown away. However, nothing can disguise the magnificence of Adam's library, just about as fine a neo-classical interior as you will see anywhere.

Probably the most famous painting on display here is Vermeer's *Guitar Player*, but it is the English portraits and landscapes – including works by Gainsborough, Reynolds, Morland and Raeburn – which are the mainstay of the collection, and most appropriate in this setting. Also do not miss Wright of Derby's *Two Girls Dressing a Kitten by*

Candlelight, unmistakable in its expressionistic lighting and questionable subject-matter. There is also some fine furniture here and there, but the great feature other than the Gainsboroughs, etc, is the extensive and well-presented collection of portrait miniatures. The relatively small scale of the room in which these are displayed makes it much easier to come to terms with the characteristics of the genre than it ever is in a normal museum. Unfortunately, the collections of rather dowdy jewellery and shoe-buckles in the same room distract one's attention from the outstanding quality of the miniatures.

There are lavatories and a small shop in the house, and a very enjoyable café in the old brewhouse round the corner. In summer, there is an evening concert series in the grounds, so you might want to time your visit so as carry on afterwards to listen to music and have a picnic in these incomparable surroundings.

London Canal Museum

ADDRESS 12/13 New Wharf Road, King's Cross, London N1 9RT (020 7713 0836) WEBSITE www.canalmuseum. org. uk OPEN Tuesday to Sunday and bank-holiday Mondays, 10.00–16.30. Closed, normal Mondays and some days at Christmas and New Year ADMISSION £2.50, concessions £1.25 GETTING THERE underground to King's Cross, then slightly intimidating walk (5 minutes)

Housed in a pleasant 19th-century light-industrial building in a King's Cross back street, the canal museum has some interesting material on display, but an almost terminal sense of loss of the will to live. The huge basement ice-wells have been only partially excavated, which is perhaps just as well, since there is a constant noise of running water, suggesting that total inundation is not far off. The back of the museum opens on to an agreeable canal basin, with narrowboats moored, and the canal's own small tug under restoration. On the ground floor, storyboards tell a fascinating history of the importation of ice from Norway, first by ship to Limehouse, then by barge to the numerous ice-wells situated on Battlebridge and Cumberland Basins, finally by horse and cart to restaurants and prosperous households around central London. Unfortunately, the story and the display then get sidetracked into the life of one Carlo Gatti, who ran the company that owned these particular ice-wells, and a display devoted to ice-cream – connected, one can see, to the importation of ice, but nothing directly to do with the canal at all.

The display continues with a desultory collection of canal gear, haphazardly displayed, including half a reconstructed canal boat, showing off its incredibly restricted living space.

There are fascinating storyboards here and there, including some super photographs of the coal trade on the canal, and an informative display on the working of locks, unfortunately almost entirely obscured by an intervening installation.

Upstairs – sadly not via the closed horse ramp – are the stables for the cart horses which were housed here, and some material for use by children. Some fine storyboards on the history of canals in general and the Regent's Canal in particular are complemented by a remarkable film, *Barging through London*. The unfortunate 1924 quality of this silent film and its irritatingly facetious captions are more than compensated for by glorious footage of 1924 canal life and traffic. A small shop downstairs sells some waterways gear.

Markfield Beam Engine

ADDRESS Markfield Road,
London N15 4RB
(020 8802 0680)
OPEN second Sunday of each
month, 11.00–15.00

ADMISSION free, but donations
appreciated
GETTING THERE underground to
Seven Sisters, then intimidating
walk (15 minutes, see below)

This Victorian pumping engine is not easy to get to, and the effort is only worthwhile for devotees of steam engines and sewage works, or those determined upon a strange adventure. Given the very limited opening times, it would be sensible to telephone in advance before venturing forth. As to getting there, the approaches are unwelcoming: Markfield Road runs through a small, rather depressing industrial estate, and then peters out, with no museum in sight. Don't be deterred, however, the track in front of you bends round and takes you to a modern building housing the Markfield Project, and the beam engine is in the grade-II listed Victorian pumping house next door.

The machinery itself consists of the impressive steel and cast-iron beam, pistons and (very large) wheel, which pumped 4 m illion gallons of sewage per day from 1886 until its decommissioning in 1964. Unfortunately, the engine cannot be seen under steam until money is found to repair or replace the steam generator. However, the enthusiastic volunteers who run the museum will show you a 1988 video of the engine under steam, as well as showing you proudly over the engine, and telling you all about its operation and purpose. The volunteers have great plans for establishing a much more grandiose museum based around the beam engine, and will probably try to sign you up to volunteer your labour or your funds for the project.

Royal Air Force Museum

ADDRESS Grahame Park Way, Hendon, London NW9 5LL (020 8205 2266)
WEBSITE www.rafmuseum.org. uk
OPEN daily, 10.00–18.00. Closed 25, 26 December and 1 January

ADMISSION £7.00, over-60s £5.50, 5–15s £4.50, students and unemployed £4.50
GETTING THERE underground to Colindale, then boring walk (10 minutes)

If you like looking at aeroplanes, then the slightly awkward journey out to the RAF Museum will be worthwhile: if you don't, then it won't. There are photographic displays, undistinguished paintings, historical tableaux, and a fine *son-et-lumière* show, but it is the 'planes themselves that are the point of this place. More than 70 aircraft of various sizes are distributed through the three main exhibition spaces. In the main hall, the gamut of fighting 'planes of the 20th century is presented, from a 1910 glider through to a Harrier Jump Jet. It may sound like *Boys' Own* stuff, but many of these aircraft are beautiful objects in their own right, and nearly all are extremely impressive when seen at such close quarters. Stand close to a twin-rotor transport helicopter and it has an undeniable presence. For me, the flying boats are the star attractions of this section of the museum, especially the beautiful timber hull of the Southampton flying boat of 1925–36. Throughout, brief but helpful technical and historical details of the individual craft are given, while photograph/text boards around the walls provide context. To one side, the rebarbatively named 'Fun'n'Flight' gallery has excellent interactive material demonstrating various principles of aerodynamics. These consist of refreshingly uncomputerised installations, which reminded me of the very best experimental set-ups from physics lessons in the misty past. But they really are fun to get involved with, from eye-tests to calculating windspeed, to dropping a load (i.e. bomb, I suppose, though they are too tactful to say so) from a 'plane to a target. The upper floor of the main gallery is devoted to the early years of the RAF, with photographs and tableaux (of which the one devoted to the WRAF is stupid and patronising beyond belief) from World War 1 and earlier. Back downstairs, there is an unambitious little snack bar, but you may do better to go to the café at the side of the Battle of Britain Gallery across the way.

Go through to the Bomber Hall, which is a daunting place. As you go in, you are confronted with a Lancaster bomber, and the size of the thing takes some adjusting to. But that in turn does little to prepare you for the impact of finding yourself underneath the vast sweeping delta wing of the Avro Vulcan at the rear of the hall. A truly sinister presence, in a way unmatched by any other exhibit here. In one corner of the hall, there is a rather good small installation demonstrating the effect of bombing, including a mock-up of part of a French factory bombed in 1943.

Across the car park, the Battle of Britain gallery uses some unusual curatorial effects to convey World War 2 history. The main event is a multi-media show – 'Our Finest Hour' – which combines remarkable film footage of the Blitz and the Battle of Britain with serial illumination of some of the 'planes involved in the action. Weirder by far is the Churchill waxwork delivering a speech on audiotape with lip-synched hologrammatic facial features, a technique used in another tableau in the gallery, to equally strange effect. Among the more conventional exhibits, the Sunderland flying boat is not to be missed – a massive four-engined affair that you can walk through, serving as a last reminder of how huge many of these aircraft are when encountered at close quarters.

city of london

Bank of England Museum

ADDRESS Bartholomew Lane,
London EC2R 8AH
(020 7601 5545)
OPEN Monday to Friday, 10.00–
17.00. Closed bank holidays

ADMISSION free
GETTING THERE underground to
Bank, then find the
Threadneedle Street exit

Considering the slightly unpromising nature of its subject-matter, this small museum at the back of the Bank of England does a remarkable job. The first room that you come to is a fine reconstruction of John Soane's 1793 Bank Stock Office, together with slightly disconcerting waxwork figures installed behind a counter at one end of the room. In front of the counter is a splendid recent model of the Soane buildings, which now resides permanently here following the recent touring exhibition of Soane's work. The body of the room is taken up with a collection of cartoons featuring the Bank of England and its personnel, from Gillray to Steve Bell. The latter's cartoon depicting the relationship between Eddie George, current Governor of the Bank, and the TUC is savagely hilarious. Not only is the original presented in a glass case, but it is also blown up to more than life-size and presented as a sort of tableau, dominating one end of the display area, an act revealing more élan than one might have expected. Around the walls are display cases of coins and architectural drawings. The latter are particularly interesting for J M Gandy's drawings of Soane's designs.

The second and third rooms have a tatty video of the history of the bank, but also some great archive material in glass cases, including letters of patent establishing the bank in 1694, and hand-written banknotes from around the same period. A strange fascination is exerted by the early staff-lists, giving names, job-titles and salaries: multiply the figures by about one thousand for their modern equivalents, though I think you would have to allow for a greater range at the lower end today. More seriously, there is a good deal of interesting material relating to the Bank's political and economic importance from 1694 to the present.

At the heart of the museum, the rotunda contains a display of gold bars, most of them allegedly replicas, which seems an exercise in uncharacteristic futility. Also a collection of antique silverware of some distinction and a bunch of inferior Roman artefacts. More interesting is the display of banknotes and machinery associated with their manufacture, and the startling information that six tonnes of used notes are destroyed every day in England – ground into fine particles, because burning them would have too much negative impact on the environment, or so they say.

On from the rotunda is an interactive video of monumental tedium on the make-up and workings of the Bank's Monetary Policy Committee. However, the museum immediately redeems itself with a captivating mock-up of a currency-dealing room, and a splendid currency-dealing computer game. Finally, back to the entrance, and a courtesy call on the small shop, where you can buy a bottle of Bank of England sherry, should you feel so inclined.

Dr Johnson's House

ADDRESS 17 Gough Square, London EC4 (020 7353 3745)
OPEN May to September, Monday to Saturday, 11.00–17.30; October to April, Monday to Saturday, 11.00–17.00. Closed bank holidays

ADMISSION £3, concessions £2, children 10 and over £1, under-10s free
GETTING THERE underground to Chancery Lane or Blackfriars. Bus 341 to Fetter Lane; 11 along Fleet Street

The way through to Dr Johnson's House in Gough Square is well signposted both from Fleet Street and from Fetter Lane, which is just as well since it is rather hidden in this strange little enclave of small alleys and courtyards among legal and financial offices. Perhaps the best thing about the house is the building itself. It is unusual nowadays to see a house of this age (built 1700) which is not on the grand scale. Thus one's relationship with the building is unfamiliar in its approachability, and so in its way more compelling than is the case with grace-and-favour access to larger places. There is a sense of Johnson's real life conveyed by the domesticity of this interior, even though no attempt is made to furnish the place fully. Indeed, that is one of the attractions, because the rooms are beautifully simple, and the small amount of furniture is of high quality and similarly unpretentious.

The most important aspect of the house is the library, which has unique material available for use by researchers in the Johnsonian field. Apart from that, there are a number of household bits and pieces, together with editions of Johnson's dictionary and more or less informative copies of letters and other documents on display. A game to be played here is to try to work out how many Samuel Johnsons there must have been from the pictures on the wall. The many pic-

tures on display are of – well – variable quality. To say that
no two pictures of Johnson himself are alike says much for
the originality of the painters concerned, but does give rise
to some unease as to the accuracy of one's internal image of
the man.

As to the building itself, the doorway and tiny courtyard
make for a comforting and agreeable introduction to the
place. Inside, it is definitely worth the climb up to the top
floor, to the attic room in which Johnson's clerks worked.
It is now very sparsely furnished, which allows the beautiful proportions and situation of the room to impress themselves. As one goes downstairs, each floor consists in effect
of two modest-sized rooms, each of which contains a small
number of exhibits. There is a beauty and simplicity to this
understated approach towards presentation which is
extremely effective. The building is allowed to speak for
itself, though there are also informative and worthwhile
factsheets in each room. Note in particular the hinged
screen-walls on the first floor, by means of which three
rooms can be converted into one, leaving the staircase
closed off.

The effect of this beautifully restored house risks being
vitiated by the video display, which glowers with its half
dozen seats on one of the landings. Looking down on it from
the stairway it seems quite surreal, this huge television set in
an 18th-century house. And the video show itself is a risky
effort to evoke an 18th century of full-bottomed wigs: a
waltz with the bogus which the house itself manages to
avoid, being a survival and restoration of such quality and
integrity that it doesn't require artificial aids at reconstruct-
ing the past.

Guildhall Art Gallery

ADDRESS Guildhall Yard,
London EC2P 2EJ
(020 7332 1632)
OPEN Monday to Saturday,
10.00–17.00; Sunday
12.00–16.00. Closed 25, 26
December, 1 January. (Also odd
days when weird things are
going on at the Guildhall, so
phone to check before you
set out)
ADMISSION £2.50, concessions
£1.00
GETTING THERE underground
to Bank or Moorgate (and
see below)

Think of the most conventional municipal gallery that you've ever seen, add lots and lots of money, and now take away all the visitors. Presto! You've got the Guildhall Art Gallery. Or rather, you probably haven't, because one reason that nobody goes to it has to be the near impossibility of finding the place. Normally, the little brown fingerposts that point the way to places of interest in the City are very useful: not these babies, which at the time of writing evidently point to where the gallery used to be rather than where it has been since the new building was opened in August 1999. The easiest way to get to the gallery is to take the underground to Bank, then be sure to exit to Prince's Street, walk up Prince's Street to Lothbury, turn left, note the end of Basinghall Street on your right but keep going for a few yards more, then turn right through the slightly forbidding entrance into Guildhall Yard – the entrance to the gallery is practically straight in front of you across the yard.

My guess is that the commissioning document for Richard Gilbert Scott's (note the name) new building must have included the words 'pretend that 20th-century architecture hasn't happened'. The interior functions well enough, however, and the undercroft galleries are positively agreeable in an exposed-brick-vault way. The paintings in the main un-

dercroft room tend to be sub-pre-Raphaelite, though the Lawrence portrait of Kemble as Coriolanus is worth looking at, as are the Tissot group-portrait narratives in the next room. Beside the Tissots is the well-organised and user-friendly on-screen database – definitely worth consulting. In the next small room are some really fine 19th-century English paintings, including Atkinson Grimshaw's 1884 *Thames By Moonlight*, Henry Scott Tuke's 1902 exercise in homo-eroticism, *Ruby, Gold and Malachite*, and Constable's 1829–31 *Salisbury Cathedral*. Moving up to the ground floor, there are quantities of naval portraiture and action painting, including John Singleton Copley's 1783–91 *Defeat of the Floating Batteries at Gibraltar, September 1782*, notable for its vast size if nothing else. The smaller ground-floor galleries are devoted to a collection of London paintings from the 17th century to the 20th. Among these are some fascinating narratives: I am intrigued, for example, by the chap taking the cab's number in James Holmes' 1832 *Charing Cross*, while Robert William Buss's 1841 *The Crowd* is really quite funny. Also notable in this section are W L Wyllie's spectacular *Opening of Tower Bridge 1894* and Anthony Eyton's 1975–76 *Spitalfields Window*.

Upstairs, the opulent main gallery is lined with largely undifferentiable grandiose portraits. Three rather splendid exceptions: Thomas Lawrence's 1825–27 *Richard Clark, Chamberlain of London*; Thomas Thornhill's jolly 1725–27 *Allegory of London: London, Pallas Athene, Peace and Plenty*, and Thomas Hardy's (not that one) 1787 *Brass Crosby*, apparently a rather naughty Lord Mayor.

There is no café in the gallery, despite the fact that the basement cloakroom and lavatories are large enough (and opulent enough) to stage the Lord Mayor's Ball.

Guildhall Clock Museum

ADDRESS Guildhall Library,
Aldermanbury, London EC2P 2EJ
(020 7332 1868/1870)
OPEN Monday to Friday,
9.30–16.45
ADMISSION free
GETTING THERE underground to
St Paul's, Bank, or Moorgate

This is an attempt at prophecy, since the Clock Museum is closed for a general revamp from October 2000 to April 2001. Situated in a single room on the ground floor of the undistinguished 1960s(?) building that also houses the Guildhall Library, the Clock Museum manages to present a broad selection of material in a quite small space, and still avoids feeling cluttered. The splendid collection of timepieces ranges from the 15th century to the late 20th, from long-case clocks to ultra-thin wristwatches. There are fine examples of work by the most celebrated English clockmakers, including Thomas Tompion and John Harrison (who invented the first reliable marine chronometer).

Although much of the collection will be of greatest interest to the specialist, there are also many items which display considerable craftsmanship and some beauty, also some items of historical interest, such as the (very ordinary) wristwatch worn by Edmund Hillary on the ascent of Everest.

In view of the current closure, do phone the Guildhall Library to check opening times and so on before setting out. If it all goes horribly wrong, the Guildhall Art Gallery (see page 159) is only round the corner.

Museum of London

ADDRESS London Wall, London
EC2Y 5HN (020 7600 3699;
info@museumoflondon.org.uk)
WEBSITE www.museumoflondon.
org.uk
OPEN Monday to Saturday,
10.00–17.00; Sunday,
11.30–17.50

ADMISSION £5, concessions £3,
16 years and under, disabled and
assisters free. Free to all after
16.30. NB All tickets are valid
for return visits for one year
GETTING THERE underground to
Barbican, Moorgate or St Paul's.
Buses 8, 11, 15, 23, 25

The unprepossessing 1970s grey and black exterior of this
building shares with other parts of the Barbican development an apparent disinclination to admit access. But perse-
vere, follow the signs, and you will get there, eventually.
Once inside, it is odd how a comparatively simple lay-out
succeeds in being really quite confusing, so pick up a free
plan. Leaving aside for the moment the temporary exhibition space which you first encounter, the permanent collection is arranged roughly chronologically from 500,000 BCE
to the present, in a descending spiral. The prehistoric material is organised in child-oriented tableaux, and is absolutely
fascinating for anyone who doesn't already know this stuff.
The problem is that an auroch is an auroch, whether or not
its thigh-bone was discovered in the Thames Valley. (Though
there is something faintly endearing – at least to north Lon-
doners – about a collection of neolithic doo-dahs whose site
of discovery is described as Stoke Newington, depicted in all
its rural primeval glory in the painting at the back of the display case. The residents haven't changed a bit.)

With the Roman displays, you begin to acquire a sense of
the past's relation to London as it is today, and this sense is
reinforced by the constant renewal of the display of the most
recent archaeological finds. This perhaps buttresses a kind

of temporal parochialism in which I think many of us operate, and so the displays become progressively more fascinating the nearer they come to the present. There seems to have been something of a failure of curatorial nerve here and there, so that the pride of place given to the Lord Mayor's not-terribly-interesting coach distracts the enquiring gaze from more worthwhile stuff, as does the disappointing Great Fire tableau-would-be-vivant. Another oddity is the ghastly piped noise which follows one around: imagine the aural equivalent of Morris dancing and you'll get the idea.

Do not miss the Rhinebeck Panorama, a painting of about 1807, which was discovered fairly recently in Canada, bought for the museum, and has been on display here only for the past very few years. Between the game of working out what's what from the painting, referring to the excellent key, and then being fascinated by the little scenes of everyday life incorporated into this architectural panorama, there is a danger of spending a great deal of time in front of this. Indeed, the same effect repeats itself over and again, as the detailed installations produce a telescopic effect, whereby the general pleasure imparted by shop-interiors or other installations gives way to a fascination with the detail underlying the first impression. To do all of it justice would entail spending an entire day at the museum, which is fine if you have the time to spare.

In any case, you are almost bound to spend more time here than you had planned, because the natural sequence in which to go round the museum is a chronological one, and the exhibits grow more and more fascinating as one comes nearer to the present, especially to items remembered from one's youth. It was the Cortina Mark 1 that transfixed me, but most of us will be equally susceptible to something in the

show. The World War 1 and 2 installations are worthwhile, incorporating some interesting photographic and other material. But then, the 20th-century stuff is generally captivating – photographs, storyboards, and physical exhibits. There is an utterly compelling model of a couple of Hackney streets – 'London Fields – The Ghetto', by James MacKinnon and Tom Hunter – which invites the viewer into an intimate look at domestic and shop interiors and exteriors.

For all its fascination, there is a problem with the 20th-century material in that there is a distinct feeeling that the museum cannot decide what to include and what to leave out. Even with a regular rotation of exhibits, there is a sense of clutter – and to do full justice to what is on display then begins to feel like quite hard work. As to the temporary displays, these seem to be curated with a disregard for reality which is quite startling. A recent small installation consisted almost entirely of a rant against planners and pedestrianisation schemes: a truly extraordinary stance to take in a city which is suffering from motorised arterio-sclerosis to the extent that London is.

The shop is quite good, in that it has some sensible books on display, though some of the other material looks, as usual, as though it had come from English Heritage Central Supplies. But food is a real problem. The café which is marked on the museum plan is actually a separate enterprise across the walkway outside. The curse which follows me around where lunch is concerned has here resulted in a score during recent visits of 1. elderly sandwich resulting in distinctly queasy feeling; 2. café closed; 3. café closed down. But it may be ok by now. In any case, you can always walk round to the Barbican Centre for a snack.

Museum of the Order of St John

ADDRESS St John's Gate,
St John's Lane, London
ECIM 4DA (020 7253 6644)
OPEN Monday to Friday,
10.00–17.00; Saturday,
10.00–16.00. Tours on Tuesday,
Friday, Saturday, 11.00 and 14.30
ADMISSION free. Tours £4.00,
elderly £3.00
GETTING THERE underground
to Farringdon, then walk
(5 minutes)

You might want to time your visit so as to enable you to combine the museum with a tour of the headquarters of the Order – the English Branch of the Knights Hospitallers – taking in the restored and reconstructed 12th-century Priory Church as well as the Tudor gatehouse and tower.

In the museum itself, much of the material devoted to the history of the Order tends to be geared towards an insider's point of view, rather obscure medals and uniforms and so on. However, there are the most lovely Maltese majolica pharmacy jars from the 16th to the 18th centuries, when Malta was the home of the Knights Hospitallers. There is also a small room devoted to 16th- and 17th-century armour, and another with sundry archaeological finds. One magnificent thing here is a smallish, perhaps 40 cm by 3 metres, 15th-century carved and painted wooden panel.

The shift in mood as you go into the permanent exhibition devoted to the work and history of the St John Ambulance is jarring, but embodies the contradictions of an organisation steeped in quasi-mystical history on the one hand while having an important role in modern healthcare on the other. This part of the museum is presented as a modern installation, with videos and informative storyboards. Film footage and photographs from World Wars 1 and 2 are fascinating, and there is useful glass-case material on the development of stretchers and other first-aid equipment.

The tour of the premises lasts about an hour and a quarter, and includes the pleasing church, of whose history little is now visible following World War 2 bombing and reconstruction. The cloister garden is delightful, however. Much more survives of the gatehouse, dating from 1504, with material tracking the Knights' Hospitallers' history from their origins during the Crusades, through their subsequent international roles in crusading warfare and healthcare, controlled successively from Jerusalem, Cyprus, Rhodes, Malta and Rome. There is a splendid Jacobean staircase with moulded plasterwork, and fine Maltese and French furniture, especially of the 16th to 18th centuries. The library has many fine bindings, and contains archive material available to scholars by arrangement.

St Bartholomew's Hospital Museum

ADDRESS West Smithfield,
London ECIA 7BE
(020 7601 8152)
OPEN Tuesday to Friday,
10.00–16.00. Closed public
holidays. Tours 14.00 on Fridays

ADMISSION free. Tours £4.00,
concessions £3.00, accompanied
children free
GETTING THERE underground to
Farringdon, then walk
(5 minutes, but see below)

Underfunded, threatened with closure, it seems the one thing that Bart's Hospital is not short of is history, having been founded in 1123. To get the full story of the 18th-century hospital and church buildings, the Hogarth murals and the 12th-century neighbouring church of St Bartholomew-the-Great, you may find the guided tour useful. Otherwise, the museum is quite something in its own right.

As with other London medical museums, the display here of 18th- and 19th-century medical instruments is gruesome but fascinating. A volume of reproductions of 19th-century illustrations of fearsome ailments adds to the general queasiness. Alongside some fine 18th-century apothecaries' gear is an extensive storyboard installation on Bart's role as a teaching hospital, and particularly its contribution to the professionalisation of nursing. There is also a pair of weird audio installations, which seem to be a nod in the direction of interactivity.

What is unusual about the Bart's display is the age of some of the archive material. On display are documents relating to the foundation of the hospital going back to 1137, and the seals on some of the 12th- and 13th-century documents are in remarkably good condition – quite a sigillophile's delight. The other major attractions here are the Hogarth murals on the 18th-century staircase. Viewing conditions are not ideal, as visitors to the museum are penned in one corner of the bottom landing to the staircase, but the vantage point still affords a sufficient view of the murals to get the general idea. *The Good Samaritan* is the less visible of the two, but *The Pool of Bethesda* (1734–37) is spectacular – the more so since the museum provides a handy key to the revolting diseases from which the characters seeking Christ's healing are suffering.

Finding the museum is not entirely straightforward. The West Smithfield entrance to the Bart's complex consists of an elongated archway, almost a tunnel. Go through this into a courtyard, across the courtyard into another archway. The museum entrance is on the left of the inside of this second archway.

east london

Bethnal Green Museum of Childhood

ADDRESS Cambridge Heath
Road, London E2 9PA
(020 8983 5201)
OPEN Saturday to Thursday,
10.00–17.50

ADMISSION free
GETTING THERE underground to
Bethnal Green. Buses 106, 253,
309, D6

This is childhood on the large scale, housed in a mid-19th-century galleried building which apparently formed part of the original temporary structure that subsequently became the Victoria & Albert (see page 50). The childhood theme perhaps embraces too large a field for its own good, and it may be more useful to approach this as a glorified toy and game museum. That is not to discard, for example, the clothes from the 17th century to the present, but they do seem a barely relevant adjunct to the main event, and I was the only person in that part of the museum when I was there. Throughout, the bulk of the museum is devoted to glass-case material, well-enough presented, with well-spaced cabinets, not unduly cluttered. More signage might be useful.

Tripping through the toys, then, the top floor has a substantial and thoughtful exhibition of 'Learning Toys', with items from 300-year-old miniature furniture to Montessori and other late-20th-century stuff. Curiously, learning toys in the mass seem to be about training children to be adults rather than how to be better children. My favourite item here was a set of miniature curling stones, an idea that I loved until I put on my glasses and they turned out to be bells.

Down to the Upper Ground floor, where there are some hundreds of dolls from the 17th century to the present. While the emphasis is on British, American and German dolls, there has been a worthwhile attempt to achieve exam-

ples from around the world. Also on this floor are games –
chess, draughts, Monopoly, much what you would expect.
Except that then you come across an entire cabinet devoted
to different versions of Lotto, including the charmingly
refined 'Floral Lotto'. Perhaps the best things are the illustrations on the outside of the boxes, from the rather
naughty-looking Edwardian 'Hopla! Edition de Luxe' to the
wholesome 1950s children, universal on boxes of the
period. A cultural historian could have a field day ...

The section devoted to toy theatres includes a magnificent
18th-century Italian number, and there are marionettes,
glove puppets and shadow puppets. Moving on, there is a
fine range of bears, and cth r stuffed toys from golliwoggs
to Teletubbies. Locomotives and railway set-ups give way to
miniature shops from the 1850s to the 1970s. Particularly
fine are the elaborate Noah's Arks from 1810 to 1990.

Down on the lower ground floor are the dolls' houses.
These are quite magnificent, nearly 50 of them dating from
the 17th century to the 1950s. But they are more interesting
as architectural and social records than as playthings: indeed
most of them were obviously never intended as children's
toys, and again one wonders if the museum has slightly lost
its sense of direction.

The lower ground floor also contains a modest café and a
small shop.

Geffrye Museum

ADDRESS Kingsland Road,
London E2 8EA (020 7739 9893)
WEBSITE www.geffrye-museum.
org.uk
OPEN Tuesday to Saturday,
10.00–17.00; Sundays and bank-
holiday Mondays, 12.00–17.00.
(Note: closed on normal
Mondays)
ADMISSION free
GETTING THERE buses 67, 149,
242 or 243

The Geffrye Museum is situated on a stretch of Kingsland Road which, refreshingly seedy, continues for the moment to resist the garish move upmarket in Hoxton and Shoreditch to its immediate south and the gentrification that has now almost completely taken over the early 19th-century houses to its north. Converted from a group of 18th-century almshouses, the museum is devoted to urban domestic interiors, and there is something not quite respectable about it. One of the facets of this is embodied in dripping autumn trees in its forecourt, a silence and an absence of people, weirdly separate from the traffic on Kingsland Road on the other side of the railings. This is melancholic and beautiful, but takes some effort to capture, since most of the time the museum's outgoing approach to securing children as enthusiastic visitors is reflected in a cheery tumult. And therein lies another aspect of the place that is not quite respectable. For, although a disproportionate number of the child visitors are, of course, fresh-faced scions of the Hackney middle-classes, there are also quite a lot of kids here who look to be from rough backgrounds, and who would probably be shown the door at many museums. Incidentally, the Geffrye manages to combine a welcoming face towards children with an extremely helpful and scholarly approach to serious enquiries about cabinet-making history.

When there are not very many visitors around, you will

probably think that the place is shut: this is either because you have come on a Monday and it really is shut, or because the entrance is at one corner, and not in the middle, where the closed double doors look forbidding. Once you have found your way in, however, the staff are generally welcoming and helpful, and entrance remains free.

For the most part, the exhibits take up one side of a long corridor, and consist of a string of sitting-rooms, set out with the furniture and decor of their period, chronologically from the late 16th century to the 1990s. (Because the amount of space within which you can move is quite restricted, be prepared to be patient with children and slow-moving people.) Throughout, there are display panels which place these interior cameos in their economic and geographical urban context. In addition there are two welcoming reading rooms, a small, elegant one forming a sort of bay-windowed passageway overlooking the herb garden, and the other in the main part of the building, the latter being rather devoted to children. Further on, in the extension, there is a superb interactive database, great fun to play with.

The southern end of the museum is housed in a new extension, which opened in 1998. The Branson Coates design is a quite pleasing stone, metal and glass ensemble. However, I am always a bit suspicious of anything that has been opened by the Prince of Wales, as this was, and it leaves me thinking that a design that worked less hard at being sympathetic to its surroundings and to the pre-existing structure, and splashed more into the area of the innovative carbuncle might have been better. I am also prejudiced because it is in the new wing that the Geffrye makes its bid for a respectability which I think it would do better to shun.

The new restaurant is a pleasant but undistinguished tent-

like structure in steel and glass with stone-flagged floor. The menu is short but quite sensible and reasonably-priced, and the service is well-meaning but decidedly eccentric. But note that word 'service'. It seems a bit schizophrenic for a museum to have on the one hand an outreach policy which is so clearly successful at bringing in local children, while on the other hand the only place in the museum in which it is apparently possible to secure food or drink of any description is a table-service restaurant.

After you've looked at London sitting-rooms from the 17th, 18th and 19th centuries, the new wing houses the displays devoted to 20th-century stuff. And, of course, everybody gets enthusiastic at this point, trying to remember whether Granny's armchair was the same as that one, and wondering whether one's own decor really looks quite as dodgy as *that*. Unlike the main part of the museum, the extension looks so smart that all the exhibits tend to look a bit dowdy in comparison, but that will no doubt wear off in time. In the mean time, note the small but really rather fine collection of 20th-century paintings on the wall of the room that houses the interactive monitors.

As in almost every other museum, there is a shop, and disappointingly this one looks to have been stocked from central supplies: it is absolutely indistinguishable from what you would find in an English Heritage house near Guildford. Downstairs is also a crafts gallery, where the exhibits are on sale at prices that make me rock slightly on my heels, but are probably just what one-off pieces cost anywhere. Nevertheless, this appeal to the well-to-do reinforces that sense that the Geffrye is trying to appeal to two separate and very different constituencies.

Last, do not miss the herb garden at the rear of the building. The entrance to this is even more misleading than that to the main building, being right out by the north gate at the front. But once found the garden is really lovely, a sensitive but not coy attempt to recreate the kind of planting that may have been commonplace in the gardens of wealthy 18th-century Hackney houses.

Ragged School Museum

ADDRESS 46–50 Copperfield
Road, London E3 4RR
(020 8980 6405)
OPEN Wednesday and Thursday,
10.00–17.00; first Sunday of the
month, 14.00–17.00
ADMISSION free
GETTING THERE underground to
Mile End (but see below)

The Ragged School Museum combines a small but excellent series of social-history displays with a re-creation of a schoolroom from the 1890s, when one of Dr Barnardo's ragged schools operated here. It is housed in three small interlinked warehouse buildings, and was attended, incredibly, by up to 1075 children in its heyday as a school. It is run by very nice and helpful volunteers, who talk to school parties about their experiences growing up in the east end. Although its prime function is as an educational resource for children, it is also open to the individual visitor. Unfortunately, with steep narrow staircases it is really not suitable for people with limited mobility.

The top floor has a reconstruction of a 1920s kitchen, and has displays of household goods from the early 20th century, together with storyboards and photographic displays. The first floor consists of the 1896 schoolroom, while on the ground floor there is a display devoted to the history of Tower Hamlets – storyboards and artefacts related to industry and commerce and the changing population mix of the area.

Getting to the museum is not easy, and the direction signs are not terribly helpful. From Mile End station, turn left along Mile End Road for about 150 metres until you are about to cross the canal. Do not do so, but instead turn left down the path through the park and keep going until the path takes you down to the towpath. Keep going until you come to the first of the blocks of flats on this side of the canal. There is at this point a path to the left, which takes you to the rear of the flats, across an open space to a row of semi-industrial buildings. The museum is at the far end of this row. But don't be put off by the slight difficulty of finding the place: it is well worth the effort.

Royal London Hospital Museum

ADDRESS St Augustine's with St
Philip's Church, Newark Street,
London E1 2AA
(020 7377 7000 x3364)
OPEN Monday to Friday,
10.00–16.30. Closed public
holidays
ADMISSION free
GETTING THERE underground to
Whitechapel, then as below

The London Hospital played an important role in improving
the dreadful conditions that prevailed at one time (perhaps
still) among many of the residents of the East End, and also
pioneered major developments in medical science. The
museum is quite difficult to find. Go through the main
entrance of the hospital on Whitechapel Road and head
straight ahead till you come out into a courtyard, bear right
and cross a small street called Stepney Way, where you will
see a redundant church to your right. Keep going round the
church to the back until you find the entrance to the crypt,
which is where the museum lives.

Apart from the gruesome relics that seem to dominate all
medical exhibitions – 18th- and 19th-century surgical
instruments, and horrific dental stuff and orthodontic appli-
ances – there is extensive archive material on display about
medical innovations in the hospital. Radiotherapy in particular was pioneered here, and with a cavalier disregard
for elementary safety of the practitioners which led to
their deaths.

Another area in which the London Hospital was a leader,
along with St Thomas's and Bart's (see page 171), was in the
development of the nursing profession. Eva Luckes was
matron here from 1880 to 1919, and seems to have been a
Florence Nightingale figure, a terrifying and energetic bour-
geoise who established standards by sheer force of will.
Edith Cavell trained here in the 1890s, and was no doubt

plucky. In celebration of all this, there is an installation of nurses' uniforms and equipment from 1885 to 1995.

Thanks to Hollywood, the most famous resident of the London Hospital is Joseph Merrick, immortalised on film by John Hurt in *The Elephant Man*, and there is a certain amount of archive material about Merrick on display, as well as a 50-minute video.

A selection of videos is available for viewing, including some wonderful promotional material from the 1930s, with great silent footage of the activities which underpin the operation of the hospital – cleaning and laundering and so on – interspersed with weird scenes in which a couple of doctors smoke and drink themselves into catatonia. The flippancy of the inter-war years in this country strikes a really odd note in these circumstances.

Fascinating as it is, the amount of material presented in the form of storyboards is a bit too much to assimilate easily: it's a bit like going to a museum and then being compelled to read a book. However, the London Hospital's social-reform role since its foundation in 1740 is undersung and it is well worth coming here to find out about it.

William Morris Gallery

ADDRESS Lloyd Park, Forest
Road, London E17 4PP
(020 8527 3782)
WEBSITE www.rbwf.gov.uk/wmg
OPEN Tuesday to Saturday and
the first Sunday of each month,
10.00–13.00 and 14.00–17.00.

Closed Mondays and public
holidays
ADMISSION free
GETTING THERE underground to
Walthamstow Central, then walk
(15 minutes)

The museum in this fine 1740s house is devoted to the life and works of William Morris (1834–96). Design drawings, wallpaper and textile samples and tiles are on display on the walls of nearly every room, along with display panels giving a lot of interesting factual material on Morris' life and career. Much of the fabric design and so on has acquired a sickly quality as a result of having been too much pastiched in the 1970s: nevertheless, there is a deal of attractive material. What is also attractive is the sense of Morris' energy and vitality, as he seems to have thrown himself into both his quasi-artistic pursuits and his socialism with great verve.

Less attractive is the faint air of hokum about the entire set-up. Morris' more misty-eyed idealistic statements about design and craft are somewhat vitiated by the fact that Morris, Marshall, Faulkner and Co seems largely to have been kept afloat by money inherited by Morris from his discount-broker father or borrowed from his mother. The museum, too, is almost founded on a false premise. Although this was the Morris family home from 1848 to 1856, Morris himself would have been away from it throughout most of the period, first at Marlborough, then Oxford, then living elsewhere in London, and he almost certainly contributed nothing to the decor of the place. Perhaps I'm being too censorious, the result of being exposed to too much faux medievalism, and highly crafted editions of Malory running to all of 300 copies. There is no sense of insincerity about Morris' statement that 'the most grinding poverty is a trifling evil compared with the inequality of classes', but I just wonder what first-hand experience of this comparatively wealthy man gave him the authority to pronounce on the matter.

Apart from the rooms devoted to Morris' own stuff, there is a picture gallery filled largely with Burne-Jones's. It also has a small and not very good but rare Simeon Solomon, *Return of the Prodigal Son* of 1857, and the wall-card very usefully explains Solomon's ostracism by respectable artists – including the pre-Raphaelites – following his arrest for homosexual offences in 1881. Upstairs on the landing is a beautiful moderne china cabinet of 1930 by Frank Brangwyn, and some so-so chairs by Voysey. To one side is a room devoted to Arthur Heygate Mackmurdo's Century Guild furniture, obviously influenced by Ruskin and Morris, but showing a route towards or running in parallel with art nouveau.

Books, posters and cards are on sale in the very small downstairs shop, as is some miscellaneous tat. To the rear of the house there is an agreeable though very busy park, originally the grounds of the house, and bequeathed along with it to the people of Walthamstow.

south and
south-east london

Design Museum

ADDRESS 28 Shad Thames,
London SE1 2YD
(020 7403 6933)
WEBSITE www.designmuseum.
org
OPEN Monday to Friday,
11.30–18.00; Saturday and
Sunday, 10.30–18.00.
ADMISSION £5.50, concessions
£4.00, students £4.50
GETTING THERE underground to
Tower Hill, then walk across
Tower Bridge and left along
Shad Thames (10 minutes)

While there are some wonderful things in the Design Museum's permanent collection, the quantity on display at any given moment is small, and so it isn't really worth the time and expense of making a special trip unless there is a particularly interesting temporary exhibition on. Having said that, the building itself is absolutely beautiful, a superb exercise in knife-sharp modernism of the 1950s, reconstructed in the late 1980s by Conran Roche.

On the second floor, the permanent collection is exhibited in groups of products such as chairs (lots, and largely unlabelled), radios, televisions, telephones and so on. While it is fascinating to follow the evolution of a product, there is a worrying lack of coherence in the selection of display items here. The statement of purpose on the wall tells us that 'The Design Museum Collection is devoted to the study of design for mass production'. Why, then, are there so many examples of Darwinian culs-de-sac included in the displays? Quirky, interesting, horrifying, according to the degree of self-indulgence in the design, they may be, but the more interesting theme of the evolution of genuinely mass-produced items is sacrificed in order to satisfy our taste for the meretricious.

The first-floor temporary exhibition space is darkly rectilinear: often the exhibitions here are excellent, if occasionally under-curated, as was, for example, the recent Buck-minster Fuller show. On the ground floor, the café is excellent: nice snacks, reasonably priced, and a lovely airy space with picture windows giving only moderately good views over the river. (The best view is from the terrace of Conran's far more expensive Blue Print Café which shares the building, and has bagged the better spaces. And is a lovely place for lunch, if you can afford it.) Unfortunately, the museum café isn't licensed, but at least you don't have to pay the entrance fee to the museum to go there.

Dulwich Picture Gallery

ADDRESS Gallery Road, London
SE21 7AD (020 8693 5254)
WEBSITE www.dulwichpicture
gallery.org.uk
OPEN Tuesday to Friday,
10.00–17.00; Saturday, Sunday
and bank-holiday Mondays,
11.00–17.00. Closed Monday
except bank holidays

ADMISSION £4.00, elderly £3.00,
students, unemployed and
children free. Free for everybody
on Fridays
GETTING THERE rail from
Victoria to West Dulwich, then
walk (15 minutes. Note: it's best
to ignore misleading direction
signs on the way)

The first purpose-built picture gallery in the world, a major
surviving Soane building, and a fine collection of pictures –
take your pick for a reason to make the slightly awkward
journey to the Dulwich Picture Gallery. Although it is somewhat disguised by early- and mid-20th-century extensions
and restorations, the quality and originality of the Soane
building still shine through, ironically the more so since the
self-effacing extension by Rick Mather was opened in May
2000. The natural top-lighting provided by Soane's design
creates excellent viewing conditions for the 17th- and 18th-
century paintings in the collection. And this is not just vacu-
ous camp historicism: try looking close-up at Guido Reni's
spotlit *St Sebastien* for an object lesson in how difficult and
destructive artificial lighting can be.

Before starting on the pictures proper, the mausoleum
built for Peter Francis Bourgeois is worth a look as an
example of Soane's daring juxtaposition of shapes. The
square antechamber is transformed into a circular space by
the austere columns, and the ceiling is a classic example of
Soane's shallow dome. Then the inner chamber is starkly
rectilinear, roughly a cube doubled in height. Together the
two spaces are practically a large hollow sculpture. To right

and left of the entrance to the mausoleum, the temporary exhibition spaces of rooms vii and viii are at the time of writing devoted to material related to Soane's designs for the gallery.

Now for a quick tour of the paintings. The numbering of the rooms is rather strange, so what follows is in a geographically logical sequence even though it doesn't look like it. The Poussins in room iv take on a perhaps unfamiliar aspect in the wonderful viewing conditions, which underline the quaint starkness of the figuration. In the same room, Sebastien Bourdon's *Brawl in a Guardroom* has a spirit of gloomy, grey detachment about it which is truly sinister. Next door in room v is Guido Reni's superb *St Sebastien*. As noted above, it is extremely difficult to see this picture close up because of the surface reflection from the spotlight. For those with good long-distance vision, it can be seen to good effect through two doorways from room iii: in any case, along with its neighbouring *John the Baptist*, the beauty and eroticism of the painting make it worth seeking a vantage point from which you can see the thing.

Room vi has some Tiepolos, and a superb Caracci *Head of an Old Man*, while room viii has a couple of wonderful Murillos. The label to *Two Peasant Boys and a Negro Boy* refers to Murillo's 'interest in children', which, with nine children of his own, was no doubt innocent and wholesome. Looking at these paintings, however, one can't help wondering ... Don't miss Fragonard's bizarre ugly *Young Woman* in room xii, then in the central hallway, room iii, there are some wonderful Reynolds portraits, including his bespectacled self-portrait of 1788 – compare his hard-of-hearing self portrait in Tate Britain (see pages 32–33). The 17th-century Flemish paintings in room ii include some revelatory Rubens modellos, among which the c. 1619 *Miracles of Saint Ignatius of Loyola* astonishingly foreshadows Francis Bacon. More familiar perhaps is the exuberant lactation in Rubens' *Venus, Mars and Cupid*.

Through to room xi, where Ruisdael's *Landscape with Windmills* (c. 1650) is outstanding: there is also a nice Hobbema in here, and a couple of Rembrandt portraits. Star of the show in this room, however, is Arent de Gelder's *Jacob's Dream*, a Blakeian vision, but expressed in oils in the late 17th/early 18th century.

Round the corner to rooms i and x, where, among some pretty indifferent English portraiture, the anonymous *Portrait of a* [nameless and apparently mad] *Man* is startlingly wonderful. In the neighbouring room is Gainsborough's portrait of Thomas Linley the Elder. I can't help comparing it with his portrait of J C Bach in the National Portrait Gallery (see page 110): it's not only that the two paintings are so obviously by the same hand, but they seem to be of the same man as well.

The problem for me with taking the rooms in this order is that one finishes with Dutch Italianate Landscape Painting of 1630–1670, and it is so much not my bag that I am intrigued by only one question: why on earth has the greyhound towards the centre of Adam Pynacker's *Landscape with Sportsmen and Game* chosen this particular moment to do *that*?

On from the main collection into Rick Mather's unassertive extension. An arts education centre and temporary exhibition space are grouped around a lovely glassed-in cloister. Also here are the surprisingly grubby and inadequate lavatories and the excellent café. It's fairly expensive, but has a nice lunch menu and agreeable snacks at other times. Best of all though, at the time of my last visit, was the good organisation and excellent service – lessons from here could usefully be learnt by many other museum cafés.

Fan Museum

ADDRESS 12 Crooms Hill, Greenwich, London SE10 8ER (020 8305 1441; admin@ fan-museum.org)
WEBSITE www.fan-museum.org.
OPEN Tuesday to Saturday, 11.00–17.00; Sunday, 12.00–17.00
ADMISSION varies according to temporary exhibition, but of the order £3.50, concessions £2.50. Tuesday 14.00–16.30; elderly and disabled free.
GETTING THERE rail from Charing Cross or London Bridge to Greenwich or Maze Hill; Docklands Light Railway to Cutty Sark; by boat to Greenwich Pier from Charing Cross or Westminster piers

Specialisation with a vengeance, you may think. And there is a limit to the amount of interest that most people can summon in miniature paintings with pleats across them But the setting is lovely: two adjoining Georgian houses in an elegant terrace around the corner from the National Maritime Museum (see page 211) have been converted to house this display of fans, mainly 17th–19th century. There is craftsmanship indeed in the manufacture of the fans, but something unsatisfactory about them in the mass. On the ground floor, after a series of glass-case displays of all-too-exquisite exercises in ivory and tortoiseshell carving, it comes as a considerable relief to see the semi-humorous display of modern electric fans. An audio-guide to all this is provided, but it is apparently aimed at listeners with a mental age of six. Upstairs, temporary exhibitions are revolved three times a year.

At the rear of the house is a super garden and parterre, and a very camp modern orangery, in which afternoon tea is served on Sunday and Tuesday afternoons.

Florence Nightingale Museum

ADDRESS St Thomas' Hospital, 2 Lambeth Palace Road, London SE1 7EW (020 7620 0374; curator@florence-nightingale.co.uk)

WEBSITE www.florence-nightingale.co.uk

OPEN Monday to Friday, 10.00–17.00; Saturday, Sunday, bank-holiday Mondays, 11.30–16.30. Closed Good Friday, Easter Sunday, 24 December–2 January

ADMISSION £4.80, children and concessions £3.60

GETTING THERE underground to Westminster, then 5-minute walk. (Cross Westminster Bridge, turn right into Lambeth Palace Road, then hard right into St Thomas' car park)

This small annexe to St Thomas' Hospital is devoted to the life and work of Florence Nightingale (1820–1910). The staff are helpful and informative, and the modest display space provides some illuminating insights. The exhibition consists primarily of storyboards with some fascinating contemporary drawings and photographs from different stages of Florence Nightingale's life. There is also a 20-minute audio/video installation, a number of artefacts displayed in glass cases, and a life-size tableau of a scene in a Crimean hospital.

Lionised by Victorian society, and sentimentalised thereafter, even with Lytton Strachey's attempt at debunking the myth it is still difficult to assess Nightingale's real achievement. What is clear is that it took a formidable will, strengthened no doubt by a severe attack of Christianity, for this haute-bourgeoise to defy her family and to enter what was at the time a far from respectable profession. Having exposed the appaling conditions in the Crimea, and set out to achieve some minimal hygiene, it was after her return to England that Nightingale seems really to have got down to

work. She published extensively, and agitated in the highest circles in order to establish a codified nursing practice, and to lay the foundations for what became the 20th-century nursing profession. And did all this just in time to thoroughly rule the roost from her bed for the last 16 years of her life.

There is a small shop, and research material is available for scholars.

Horniman Museum

ADDRESS 100 London Road, Forest Hill, London SE23 3PQ (020 8699 1872; enquiry@horniman.demon.co.uk) WEBSITE www.horniman.demon.co.uk OPEN Monday to Saturday, 10.30–17.30; Sunday 14.00–17.30. Closed 24–26 December and 1 January ADMISSION free GETTING THERE rail from London Bridge to Forest Hill (roughly 15 minutes) then walk (10 minutes)

The walk up from Forest Hill Station through undistinguished 1960s and 1970s housing is suddenly brightened by the sight of the clocktower of C Harrison Townsend's extraordinary 1898 building. As you arrive at the Horniman Museum you will see that the clocktower sits at one end of a wonderful façade, in a style best categorised as an art-nouveau take on classicism: however it is described, this is a beautiful exterior, worth making the journey to see. Incised into the façade, above the large and colourful mosaic panel, is the legend 'Horniman Free Museum' in large letters, an uncompromising statement of purpose to which the museum still holds.

At the time of writing it is difficult to give a comprehensive account of the museum, since much of it is under construction – an enlargement and modernisation project with a view to reopening in late 2001/02. The three main areas represented by the museum's collections and library are natural history, ethnography and musical instruments (but the Centre for Understanding the Environment and the musical instruments collection are not open at the time of writing). There is a feeling that the exhibits also represent a history of museum display, as the main natural-history gallery is filled with old-fashioned glass-fronted cases stuffed with dusty stuffed birds and things, and with dusty stuffed leg-

ends accompanying them, couched in Reithian language. But while the mode of presentation may seem old-fashioned, the animals seen thus exert a fascination of their own, as do especially the formaldehyde dissection specimens. I quote the overheard critical judgement of a passing 8-year-old, joyously passed on case after case – 'Yuk!' And another, in proud south London tones: 'Look, mummy, they're all dogs wot 'ave died.' There is a swimming-pool quality to the acoustic in this splendid barrel-vaulted gallery, so it only takes one slightly excitable person to deafen everyone.

The live specimens in the great little aquarium and the vivarium are completely captivating, with the latter in particular housing some rather beautiful creatures, sadly destined to anonymity until their labelling is restored. In addition to some spectacularly gruesome displays of invertebrates (so that's what a tapeworm looks like) the upper gallery has case upon case of fossils. Presented as they are, however, these are unlikely to convey much to anyone but a specialist in the field. In the same gallery is an extraordinary and splendid apostle clock, huge, complex, and the embodiment of mid-19th-century bourgeois solidity marooned in the midst of the skeletons and formaldehyde.

The African Worlds Gallery houses a collection of mainly African artefacts, very sensitively presented. The museum's Benin bronzes, for example, are accompanied by a non-hysterical but still critical account of the British imperialist adventures that led to their presence here.

In the basement is a reference library, freely accessible to anybody interested, and housing a considerable collection of material in the museum's specialist fields.

Until rebuilding is complete, there is no café at the

museum, only a refreshment area with vending machines. It is definitely worth taking time for a quick stroll in the Horniman Gardens next door to the museum: they have the feel of a decidedly upmarket municipal park, and have remarkable views across south London.

Imperial War Museum

ADDRESS Lambeth Road,
London SE1 6HZ
(020 7416 5000)
WEBSITE www.iwm.org.uk
OPEN daily, 10.00–18.00.
Closed 24–26 December
ADMISSION £5.50, concessions
£4.50, elderly and under-16s free

GETTING THERE underground to
Elephant and Castle (but
not recommended), Lambeth
North, Waterloo, Southwark.
Bus 1, 3, 12, 45, 53, 63, 68,
159, 168, 171, 172, 176, 188,
344, C10

The Imperial War Museum was founded to commemorate
World War 1, and the museum's forte today is very much the
two World Wars. Anyone looking for older material should
go elsewhere, perhaps to the National Army Museum (see
page 27). The approaches to the museum bode well: the
twin gun barrels which sit outside the main entrance are
simply magnificent pieces of engineering, huge, and imposing, if a bit phallic, and their juxtaposition with a segment of
the Berlin Wall bespeaks sensitivity and awareness. Once
inside, the arrangements only in part confirm this initial
impression. The ticketing arrangements seem designed to
create congestion, not to say confusion. For example, you
need to take your ticket for the main museum to a separate
desk in order to be issued with a timed ticket for the Holocaust Exhibition.

Take whatever time you have available before your Holocaust Exhibition ticket takes effect to look at some of the
machinery in the main hall. This is a glassed-in central
courtyard filled with field guns, tanks, armoured cars, and
missiles, including a V2 rocket (so big, and yet hundreds hit
London) and a replica of the bomb that did for Hiroshima
(so small). Above, fighter planes freeze, eternally about to
collide. On this ground-floor level there is an unambitious

café and an equally unambitious exhibition devoted to the Enigma code and its breakage.

The Holocaust Exhibition itself constitutes quite a large proportion of the interior of the museum, and you need to allow at least a couple of hours to go round it. It also tends to get crowded, hence the timed tickets. I can't tell whether this exhibition is any good or not, for a number of complicated reasons. Probably it aims too low, at least in its exposition of the Jews' historic role as international scapegoats. There are many video/audio installations, and a huge number of remarkable photographs. With much of the rest, one is left with the feeling that less would be more. It is not so much the centrally horrific exhibits that grab the attention, as the bizarre – the railway ticket with the legend beside it, 'Many Jews from Salonika were forced to pay for their railway tickets to Auschwitz', or the photograph of an incomprehensibly vast pile of shaving brushes. Perhaps I'm all holocausted out, but I can't get horrified by a photograph of a mass grave any more. What I can get horrified by, though, is the expressions on the faces of the ss men photographed imposing some fresh indignity on the Jews years before the inauguration of the deathcamps. I came away determined to reread Primo Levi.

On the second floor are the cool and uncrowded rooms devoted to paintings of the two world wars. The striking feature of many of the World War 1 paintings is the balletic quality of the soldiers depicted – as though they were no longer men, but elements in a design. However, there is no point in trying to single out particular paintings, because less than 5 per cent of the museum's holdings are on display at any given moment, and they are rotated frequently. You almost certainly won't be able to see Stanley Spencer's magnificent Clydeside paintings; they are huge, so the museum doesn't have space to hang them. Instead they spend almost all their lives being shunted round on loan to other galleries. The museum staff are unusually open to requests to see material held in store, so long as they are given adequate notice. To this end, there is a potentially excellent interactive catalogue, which has an infuriating touch-screen operation, unusable for at least some of us.

The lower ground floor houses the major World War 1 and 2 collections, largely traditional glass-case exhibits of uniformed figures surrounded by background material in huge quantities, and with often mutually conflicting audio installations. There is a reconstruction of a World War 1 trench, complete with bandaged figures, rats, and a pervasive sweetish smell, reproducing I dare not think what. The strong at heart can experience the Blitz Experience, while the less strong look at the magnificent collection of photographs in the 'Go To It' World War 2 Home Front exhibition. The odd thing is the lack of space devoted to conflicts since World War 2 – Korea gets its fair share, but there seems only to be one glass case apiece for Suez, the Gulf, the Falklands and so on. Which, if nothing else, helps to avoid triumphalism.

Medal enthusiasts are catered for by the Victoria and George Cross exhibition on the first floor, where there is also a strangely uncritical and quite large exhibition on covert operations.

National Maritime Museum

ADDRESS Park Row, Greenwich, London SE10 9NF
(020 8858 4422)
WEBSITE www.nmm.ac.uk
OPEN 10.00–17.00 daily. Closed 24–26 December
ADMISSION £7.50 (£9.50 including Royal Observatory), under-16s, under-18s in full-time education free
GETTING THERE rail from Charing Cross or London Bridge to Maze Hill; Docklands Light Railway to Cutty Sark; by boat to Greenwich Pier from Charing Cross or Westminster Piers. Then walk (5 or 10 minutes)

The National Maritime Museum embraces the Royal Observatory and the Queen's House (where special exhibitions are housed, and worth a look simply as a fine Inigo Jones building of 1635) in addition to the museum *per se*. All are situated magnificently in Greenwich Park, adjacent to Christopher Wren's Royal Naval Hospital of 1664–1702. The main museum presents an account of the economics and technology, art, lifestyles and people involved in Britain's sea-going past, pre- and post-empire.

Be prepared to spend quite a lot of time in the museum, and take time to find where the almost hidden cloakroom lurks at the main entrance. Also, beware the signs, which appear to indicate an absolutely unprecedented abundance of lavatories in the museum, but actually are only referring to lifts – unless the tower-block attitude towards lifts has spread so far. Do not worry, there are lavatories as well, just not so many as you first thought.

The museum's exhibits are divided into 16 separate permanent exhibitions, covering topics from 'Explorers' to 'The Future of the Sea'. What each of these exhibitions has in common is loud, distracting, and often mutually conflicting audio/video installations. I'm not sure that people come to

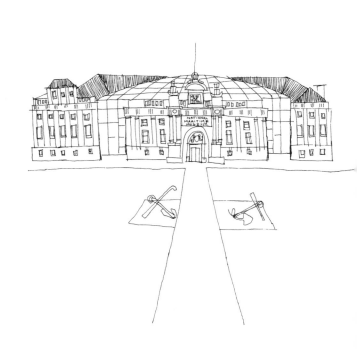

museums for what amounts to a television show, the attention being wholly and unavoidably directed, the decision having already been taken as to the relative importance of what's on show. This is a serious problem, and one which would admit of easy partial resolution simply by turning the sound down. Given that this is a national or international museum, and in every other respect is obviously very professionally presented, it is bizarre that nobody has even spotted that in some cases the noise from neighbouring audio installations renders both unintelligible.

In the central courtyard – recently rather beautifully provided with a glass canopy roof (Eiffel, 1997–99) – there are a number of quite fantastic installations in between the exhibition galleries. These are large-scale objects, ranging from Prince Frederick's barge of 1732, a confection of gilding and Grinling Gibbons carving, to a space telescope. The imaginative scope of which the museum is capable is on display in the informative and worthwhile wall panel on naval architecture, which contrives to make the leap on to dry land, a fairly obvious imaginative leap in the case of the Sydney Opera House and the Guggenheim, Bilbao, with the naval connection being rather less obvious in the case of the Pompidou Centre in Paris. Also in this central space are a wonderfully sculptural ship's propeller, and a fascinating 19th-century ship's engine.

There is a superb exhibition on passenger liners, perhaps a bit defensively nostalgic in tone, but capturing what is now a lost world. Included here is some great film footage of the 1950s, advertising ocean travel, and it is only the excessive volume to which the soundtrack has been turned up that makes it at all easy to leave this part of the museum. Moving up a floor, the 'Art and the Sea' exhibition is a

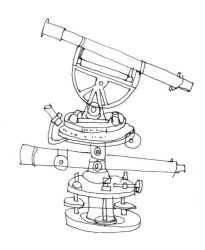

strange collection of maritime paintings: some few are out-standing – Cornelis Claesz van Wieringen's 1619 *Heemskerk's Victory Over the Spaniards at Gibraltar, 25 April 1607*, for example – while the bulk are indifferent. Somehow, the wrong note is struck here, as though the museum were aggressively asserting its right to an aesthetic sensibility which it just does not possess, (though the video installation of John Grierson's 1929 *Drifters* is superb). What it does do effectively and sensitively, however, is to point out the extent to which many of these works of art were exercises in nationalistic propaganda.

Moving on, the 'Seapower' gallery contains some super scale-models, together with a hands-on installation of control panels from a frigate and an almost full-scale submarine interior. Curiously, it is the photographs of shipboard life and of the dockyard environs which have the most impact, though Richard Ernst Eurich's World War 2 narrative paintings are lovely exercises in a sort of expressionist realism. To one side of the Seapower Gallery is the decent-enough main café and restaurant. Still on the first floor, and moving back to the roof of the central gallery, there is a more modest but rather nice café, with the sky seeming to flow past on the other side of the canopy roof, and the space generally captivating, the surrounding exhibits being on the large scale and such as to provide the essence of a really well-designed sculpture park.

Up another level to the Bridge and the children's interactive gallery, where some great hands-on games attract children of all ages. (Adults may find the instructions for playing the games exiguous to the point of incomprehensibility.)

The largest gallery is devoted to Lord Nelson, as you would expect. Here there is a large and quite impactful collection of paintings, artefacts, memorabilia – and audio/ video installations. The marvellous Turner painting *The Battle of Trafalgar* has a raucous commentary blaring away beside it.

People with children could happily spend a full day here. For the rest of us, it is essential to leave plenty of time to visit the Royal Observatory (see page 222), a brisk and splendid uphill walk away through Greenwich Park.

Museum of Garden History

ADDRESS Lambeth Palace Road, London SE1 7LB (020 7401 8865; info@museum gardenhistory.org)
WEBSITE www.museumgarden history.org
OPEN February to mid-December, Sunday to Friday, 10.30–17.00
ADMISSION free
GETTING THERE underground to Westminster, then 10-minute walk. (Cross Westminster Bridge, then turn right along Embankment to Lambeth Palace)

This is not really a museum in the conventional sense, more of a refuge from the realities of London life. From the agreeable knot garden, through the redundant church that houses the museum, to the Morris 1000 convertible parked outside, there is a faint sense of self-parody about the whole place, as if the Moreton-in-Marsh Women's Institute had set up a London branch. The unreality of the establishment is neatly encapsulated or inspired by the inscription on the tomb of Admiral Bligh, which provides an impressive focus to the knot garden: 'the celebrated navigator who first transplanted the bread fruit tree from Otaheite to the West Indies'. Mutiny? *Bounty*? No, no.

The knot garden to the rear is delightful, with parterre, high brick walls, and a lovely array of English cottage garden plants, together with some unexpected exotics; the simpler garden in the graveyard at the front is also very pleasant, especially with the surviving fine early 19th-century tombs. The church building is a pleasant enough 19th-century structure with a 14th-century tower.

As to the museum display, there is a good installation devoted to Gertrude Jekyll (1843–1932) – photographs, garden plans, letters, and a model of her own garden at Minstead Wood. There is also a display devoted to the lives of the Tradescants, gardening father and son of the late 16th and early 17th centuries, of tradescantia fame. As well as being epoch-making gardeners and importers of plants, the Tradescants were also collectors of curios from around the world. Their collection formed the core of that built up by Elias Ashmole, furnishing what subsequently became the Ashmolean Museum in Oxford with its material. Garden tools from the 18th century to the present form the bulk of the rest of the stuff on display. Some of these are extraordinary, but most are quite familiar looking – this is decidedly not an area in which technology has been moving uncomfortably fast. Otherwise, the museum has temporary displays devoted to commercial 'art' on horticultural themes, as well as a small shop, and an unambitious café.

Old Operating Theatre Museum and Herb Garret

ADDRESS 9a St Thomas' Street,
London SE1 9RY
(020 7955 4791)
WEBSITE www.thegarret.org.uk
OPEN daily, 10.30–17.00. Closed
15 December–5 January

ADMISSION £3.25, concessions
£2.25, children £1.60.
GETTING THERE underground to
London Bridge. (Exit to Borough
High Street, turn right and right
again)

Perhaps the most remarkable feature of the old operating theatre is the fact that it was forgotten about and then rediscovered (in 1957), here in the attic of the former chapel of St Thomas' Hospital. The self-consciously gruesome note struck is slightly off-putting, not because of its gruesomeness, but because it smacks of publicity-seeking. Having said that, this small museum mounts a worthwhile display, which conveys a brief history of medicine. The bunches of herbs in the herb garret confer a distinctly aromatic atmosphere on the whole enterprise, and the labelling of the displays is intelligent. Some of the extracts from the accounts of St Thomas' Hospital are intriguing: '1605 Bath of Herbs and Sheep Heads for Woman suffering from unknown illness', and '18 November 1610 Pickle herringues etc. for a poore man's feet'.

The reason for locating the operating theatre in the attic of the hospital church was probably to isolate the noise (the nature of which doesn't really bear thinking about). The operating table is little more than a slab of wood with an angled headrest, and hygiene was based around the properties of oilcloth and sawdust. Apart from the sawdust box on the floor, there was a 3-inch layer of sawdust underneath the floorboards, thus ensuring 'that any blood which reached the floor was absorbed before it could pass into the church below'.

Regular talks are given, mainly aimed at children. There are storyboards devoted to aspects of the history of surgery, and a display of 18th–20th century surgical and particularly obstetric instruments which is quite enough to put you off your lunch. Access to the museum is via a narrow winding staircase – not a practical proposition for anybody with limited mobility. Some may prefer the larger and less sensationalised display in the Hunterian Museum (see page 94).

Royal Observatory

ADDRESS Greenwich Park, London SE10
OPEN daily 10.00–17.00 24–26 December)
ADMISSION £5.00 (£9.50 including National Maritime Museum), under-16s and under-18s in full-time education free

GETTING THERE rail from Charing Cross to Maze Hill; Docklands Light Railway to Cutty Sark; by boat to Greenwich Pier from Charing Cross or Westminster piers. Steep uphill walk from the National Maritime Museum

It isn't in use as an observatory any more, and hasn't been since the 1950s, but it is a wonderful place. First of all, don't forget to turn round and look at the view once you have climbed the hill from the National Maritime Museum. But then go and be confronted with the Meridian Line, on which all lines of longitude are based globally. A brief nod at the inadequately blacked-out *camera obscura*, and then into the main building to look at a collection of quite beautiful and well-presented early navigational and astronomical instruments. (In this context, the terms navigational and astronomical are practically synonymous.) The recently reconstructed living quarters of John Flamsteed, first Astronomer Royal, present a dominant theme of clocks: even in those parts where the relationship between chronometry and navigation is clearly not the dominant theme, there still seem to be clocks in every corner. The *pièce de résistance* here is the Octagon Room, an absolutely beautiful Wren interior, with several spectacular Thomas Tompion clocks. Moving on, there is the Harrison Gallery, where the celebrated sea-going chronometers, H1 to H4, are kept – H4 oddly not kept going, in common with a number of others.

On to the Meridian Rooms, whose instruments are impressive, but whose explanatory wall-panels just don't quite say enough for the non-specialist. Lastly, to the Telescope Dome, still perfectly capable of inducing a sense of awe, as well as a chill – those guys must have felt it jolly nippy some of those winter nights tracking heavenly bodies. But it is terrific, a quite Tintinesque sense of what an observatory ought to be like.

Inevitably, the way out leads through a shop, which has a worthwhile selection of books for both adults and children as well as some pretty indifferent souvenir tat, including an unexpectedly large number of unpriced bottles of 'Greenwich Meridian' gin, whisky, and vodka. So that's what these astronomers get up to in their spare time.

Shakespeare's Globe Exhibition

ADDRESS Bankside, London
SE1 9DT (020 7902 1500)
OPEN daily, May to September,
9.00–12.00; October to April,
10.00–17.00
ADMISSION exhibition and
theatre tour £7.50, concessions
£6.00. Exhibition only £5.00,
concessions £4.00
GETTING THERE underground to
Mansion House or St Paul's then
over the Millennium Bridge, or
to Southwark and 10-minute
walk

This barely qualifies as a museum, but is just too interesting to leave out. The reconstruction of the Elizabethan Globe Theatre was completed in the late 1980s/early 1990s, using building techniques identical to those that would have been used originally – oak posts and beams fixed with wooden pegs, a hammered earth floor with hazelnut shells for drainage, and so on. Rumbustious Shakespeare productions take place during the summer afternoons and evenings. Before these performances, the theatre is open for guided tours, and there is also a large exhibition space devoted to the Shakespearean theatre.

The exhibition itself is curiously spread out around a deserted central space. It appears to be primarily aimed at children, with lots of detail on costume-making and the role of musical instruments, much of it fascinating. There are also tableaux from the Elizabethan backstage. Best of all, though, are the interactive video installations, which aim to boost your knowledge of publishing and performance in the Elizabethan period.

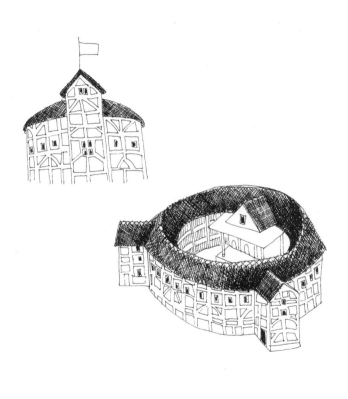

Tate Modern

ADDRESS Bankside, London
SE1 9TG (020 7887 8000;
information@tate.org.uk)
OPEN Sunday to Thursday,
10.00–18.00; Friday, Saturday,
10.00–22.00
ADMISSION free

GETTING THERE underground to
St Paul's and then walk over
Millennium Bridge (if it's open),
or to Southwark and then walk
to Bankside at Blackfriars
Bridge, ignoring misleading
signs en route

Since Tate Modern's opening in May 2000, it has constantly been packed with people, stretching its infrastructure to breaking point. One million came in the first six weeks – of course that figure includes some of us visiting more than once, but still. The Millennium Bridge must be *the* way to approach the gallery. Having crossed the river, do not use the entrance immediately in front of you, but instead turn right, and then enter the gallery using the vast ramp that constitutes the west entrance. This takes you into the Turbine Hall, a huge and beautiful space which justifies the licence given to Herzog and de Meuron when designing the conversion from power station to art gallery. Until at least 2005, this 155 metres long by 35 metres high room will be devoted to a new sculptural installation each year. It is a wonderful introduction to a splendid though not uncontroversial gallery.

At the sides of the Turbine Hall are lavatories, cloakroom, information counter, study room and shop. If you know what you want to see but don't know where it is, then instantly make use of either the information counter or the Clore Study Room. This is essential because the gallery's policy of adopting a thematic, achronological approach to siting the collection presents real difficulties. For example, suppose you want to see the Tate's holdings of Mondrian, then having looked at the printed plan, you would go to the Mondrian Room on level 5, and be rather disappointed. There is simply no indication that two important Mondrians are hung in the 'Rethinking Landscape' room on level 3. The information staff know about this problem and will help you find the works of artists scattered in improbable-sounding places. Additionally, the Clore Study Room is open to the casual visitor, though this fact is not obvious. There is an on-line catalogue here, but it is slow and operates in a curiously counter-intuitive way, so it may be best to ask the person on duty for help.

The building has seven floors, all but the sixth open to visitors. These are linked by the hopelessly over-subscribed lifts, by a wooden staircase, and escalators between levels 1 and 3, 3 and 4, and 4 and 5. Taking it from the top, level 7 houses the overstretched restaurant (less ambitious than the Tate Millbank restaurant, reasonable prices for food and wine, but queues frequently of an hour for a table, no reservations possible) and the quiet East Room, in which it is usually possible to buy a bottle of water or lemonade, and to enjoy the wonderful view. Down to level 6, which houses the Members Room, then to level 5 in which are the 15 galleries collectively designated 'History/Memory/Society' and the 14 of 'Nude/Action/Body'. Level 4 has a small espresso bar and shop, and is otherwise devoted to special exhibitions – roughly speaking, huge concatenations of small objects, as opposed to the small concatenations of huge objects that take place in the Turbine Hall. On this floor there are also a couple of external balconies providing great views across the river and much relief for desperate smokers. Level 3 houses the 14 'Landscape/Matter/Environment' rooms and the 15 called 'Still Life/Object/Real Life'. Level 2 is the level at

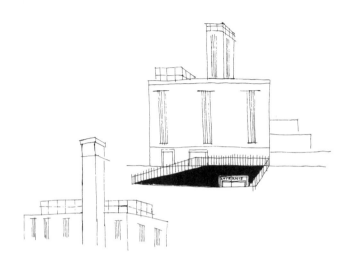

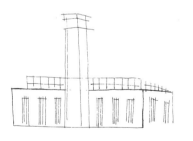

which you enter from the river via the north entrance, and has the main café – often with huge queues – small shop, and viewing gallery for the Turbine Hall, which takes us back down to level 1, with its excellent large shop, successfully combining stack 'em high souvenirs with a serious stock of books and images.

Throughout, the unvarnished wooden floors are comfortable and easy on the eye – so far – similarly, the beautiful slightly arched benches in most rooms serve as assertions of serious design values. There are lavatories on every floor except 6, and travel by escalator is painless as long as you are going to a floor served by an escalator. However, the building is something of a victim of its own success, and there are pinch points, caused by a crazy installation policy, like displaying Sam Taylor-Wood's video installation across a main thoroughfare. But there are also restful spaces, well thought-out places to sit in comfortable chairs and consult copies of the *Tate Modern Handbook* (£17 to buy, and possibly even worth it), or to enjoy the view across the Turbine Hall.

The permanent collection alone occupies 58 rooms/galleries – there is no way of doing justice to them either on a single visit or in a descriptive guidebook entry. Some things work exceedingly well. The Rothko Room (level 3) is a triumph, with the black, rust, maroon and grey paintings hung against grey walls with daringly low light levels, the whole disclosing an oppressive introspection and yet a breadth of vision in the paintings which is revelatory. Again, though, you need to ask questions before you can locate the other Rothkos in the Tate's collection (in the 'Nature into Action' room on level 3 at the time of writing). Close to the Rothko Room, do not miss the wonderful Frank Auerbach paintings, beautifully spaced, and hung in a room with light effectively diffused from the ceiling light-boxes and the windows. This lighting combines with perfect unobtrusive grey walls and the unvarnished wood floors to allow a painting such as *Oxford Street Building Site 1* of 1959–60 the quiet space needed to convey its qualities as a masterpiece.

So far as paintings are concerned, the single-artist hangings are generally unproblematic – the Bridget Riley, Stanley Spencer or whoever rooms. And I have never seen Francis Bacon hung to such good effect as his *Triptych – August 1972* on level 5: incidentally, do observe the view out over the Turbine Hall at this point, where some of the industrial kit has been left in place to serve as a giant airborne sculpture, impressive to a degree.

The themed rooms introduce the distraction of worrying about what the rationale behind a given theme might be and whether I agree with it. It detracts from the capacity of the paintings to speak for themselves. Take, for example, the room 'Modern Art in Conflict' (level 5), where the war theme is apparent, and the David Bombergs are really impressive, but why leave such a tiny sampling of German Expressionists to struggle to, er, express themselves here – which they cannot do effectively in this environment?

The three-dimensional installations have benefited more from Tate Modern's birth than have the paintings. There are still some problems, like the hazardous pinch point between the Joseph Beuys installations on level 3, but the installations themselves are wonderful and impressively displayed. Do not miss the room called 'The Perceiving Body' on level 5, in which Robert Morris' plate-glass *Untitled* (1965/71) and fibreglass *Untitled* (1967–68) are presented to intriguing, unsettling effect, as impressive a space for Morris' work as any that I have seen since his exhibition a few years ago in

the now defunct SoHo Guggenheim. The same room contains Richard Serra's wonderful *Trip-Hammer* (1988), Donald Judd's *Untitled* works of 1972 and 1990, and Carl Andre's *Venus Forge* of 1980. Anywhere else, there would (or should) be queues round the block to see modern sculpture of this importance so well presented. Here, it's another of the 58 rooms housing the permanent collection.

Two other things not to miss are the enchanting group of Giacomettis, oddly juxtaposed with Barnett Newmans in the two artists' eponymous room on level 5, and the gallery entitled 'Structures for Survival', which presents some of the strangest (and most off-puttingly titled) works in the whole museum: G-Plan meets Hammer Horror in Andrea Zittel's *A–Z Comfort Unit with Special Comfort Features by Dave Stewart* (1994–95), while Mario Merz's 1977/85 *Do We Turn Round Inside Houses or Is It Houses which Turn Around Us* is an extraordinary semi-skeletal igloo of stone, iron and glass – fractured shapes composed into a coherent but threatening whole.

That this is one of the three or four most important galleries of modern art in the world is beyond question. Unfortunately, an awful lot of other people think so too, and the infrastructure of the place cannot entirely cope. But it is a gallery which succeeds in capturing some kind of millennial spirit without unseemly posturing, and you cannot, must not, miss it.

index

Index